THE FORGOTTEN ART
OF CREATING AN OLD-FASHIONED
FAMILY
CHRISTMAS

Doing Things Together — From the Initial Hunt
for Greens to Trimming the Tree on Christmas Eve

by Barbara Radcliffe Rogers

YANKEE, INC.
Dublin, New Hampshire

Designed by Carl Kirkpatrick
Illustrated by Ray Maher

Yankee, Inc., Dublin, New Hampshire 03444
First Edition
Second Printing, 1981
Copyright 1981, by Yankee, Inc.
Printed in the United States of America

•

•

Library of Congress Catalog Card Number: 81-50535
ISBN: 0-911658-30-0

DEDICATION

To my mother, who has always
remembered Christmas and kept it magic.

CONTENTS

FOREWORD

There is a special aura that surrounds the Christmas season — a medley of lingering memories of sounds, smells, sights, and dreams; an assortment of feelings held together and made magic by the joy of giving. The gifts we present each Christmas, in remembrance of the three gifts brought to the Holy Child, are as varied as ourselves. Some we offer consciously, wrapped in bright paper; others we give unknowingly — the gifts of laughter, time, thought, beauty, joy, and love.

Christmas is a special season for our family, and its spirit extends far beyond this house and farm to family and friends nearby and across great distances. Many people have shared our Christmases, working with us, teaching us skills, and sharing ideas. And each has become a part of our permanent holiday lore. "Nana's Yulecake" and "Aunt Joan's Spice Rope" are names that will last, forever attached to the gifts that they represent.

My thanks go to all these people who've made this book possible by sharing their talents, ideas, and time: to Joan

Keenan Farrel, Pat Greene, Tillie Sobieski, Mary Plaut, Shirley Radcliffe, and Margaret, Terry, and Claire Rogers. Appreciation goes also to a group at St. James Church in Keene, New Hampshire, who have shared skills and ideas as we've worked on our annual bazaar, especially to Brenda Sherwin, Joan D'Alessio, Emma Rutherig, and Bonnie Gibbons, whose designs are shown in this book.

Clara Galante is that rare teacher who will shuffle schedules and find time for "just one more" project before Christmas. She and her classroom of talented first and second graders at St. Joseph Regional School, also in Keene, are the craftsmen who made possible the chapter on gifts for children to make.

My special thanks go to my own family — my mother and father, who taught me the first basic skills and gave me the appreciation of things handmade; Tim, who shares in so many of the projects and who built the house we so lovingly deck each season; Julie, whose enthusiasm never flags and who is an accomplished craftsman at the age of nine; and Lura, in whose eyes gleam alternately excitement and mischief and who keeps us constantly reminded of what Christmas is all about.

B.R.R.

A HIKE IN THE WOODS

Fig. 1-1. Pitch Pine

PREPARATIONS for Christmas have to begin long before snow flies. An early snow covers things on the forest floor — pine cones, partridgeberry, and teaberry — and makes the bittersweet hard to reach, so it is best to search out all these things early in the season.

Even choosing the tree (or trees), although it won't be cut until much later, should be done well ahead of time. Because the woods look different under snow, and landmarks are gone, we tie a red ribbon to the best tree before the snow falls, just to be sure we get the right one.

On your gathering trip for materials, carry a quantity of bags — paper ones for cones, pods, and grasses; small plastic bags for plants such as partridgeberry (Fig. 1-2) and teaberry (Fig. 1-3).

Both of these berry plants grow close to the forest floor, half hidden by pine needles, but their shiny leaves and red berries are not hard to spot. Along with each berry plant, dig up a little of the rich humus from the same area, and gather some moss and moist pine needles. These berry plants are the basis for terrariums and living wreaths; they will keep well if their tiny roots stay moist.

Gather every sort of cone you can find. The big, ungainly cones of the white pine (Fig. 1-4) can be used in the base of a wreath or for "fire starters." The smaller red pine, spruce, balsam, and pitch-pine (Fig. 1-1) cones are all excellent for use in wreaths and other decorations, as are hemlock cones (Fig. 1-5).

Few people are lucky enough to have such a variety of evergreens in their own back forty, but even a single tree will provide plenty of cones for a season's decorations. Among the nicest-shaped cones are those of pitch pine, a tree that is often used for landscaping. Look for it at resort areas, especially those in the mountains.

Other trees besides evergreens can also furnish decorative materials. Beechnuts, maple seeds, hickory nuts, alder catkins, acorns, and buckeyes all make handsome additions to a cone wreath. And, the sweet-gum tree has a seed that looks like a pom-pom and keeps its shape forever!

Also good for wreaths and dried arrangements are milkweed pods, evening-primrose pods, and wheat (and other) seed heads, plus heads of teasel, bergamot, tansy, cranesbill geranium, brown-eyed Susan, wild iris, and other darkened seed pods.

Although you won't cut them until later, keep an eye out for the fresh greens, too — hemlock, balsam, and cedar for wreaths, ropes, and swags, and various pines for use in vases and fruit arrangements.

Everyone has his own preference for Christmas trees. Ours is balsam. It looks and smells like a Christmas tree and is easy to decorate, being neither bushy nor prickly. Best of all, we strip the tree of its needles after Christmas to use for balsam sachets and pillows (see pp. 32-33).

Spruce also has a classic Christmas-tree shape, though it tends to be fuller than balsam. This makes it difficult to hang large ornaments that need to be placed farther into the tree rather than on branch ends. But if you favor smaller ornaments and garlands (popcorn strings, tinsel, and the like) a spruce tree is just right.

The plump and bushy Scotch pine is good for garlands. In shape, Scotch pine is more spherical than conical, and its branches are so thickly furred with spiny needles that it is nearly impossible to put lights or ornaments deep into its foliage. In addition, it scratches.

Be sure to measure from floor to ceiling before you choose a tree. Surrounded by its giant neighbors, a tree looks much smaller in the woods than it will in your living room.

Also, think about where you will put the tree and study it from all sides. If it has to go in a fairly small room, you might look for a tall, thin tree. If it has to sit right against a wall, try to find an otherwise perfect tree with one flat side.

Cut your tree as late as possible and keep its base in water at all times. Cut the trunk at a slight angle so it will have a larger absorption area, and use a firm stand with a large water basin. If you purchase a tree already cut, saw a piece off the base immediately to give it a fresh start, and keep it in water. To prolong the "life" of any tree, put it into hot water to begin with; thereafter, tap water can be used to keep the basin filled.

Your tree stand should be wide enough at the base so that the tree cannot tip over easily. This is especially important if you have small children or pets. If your floor is thickly carpeted, it is wise to put a large sheet of plywood or other firm material under the tree stand to stabilize it.

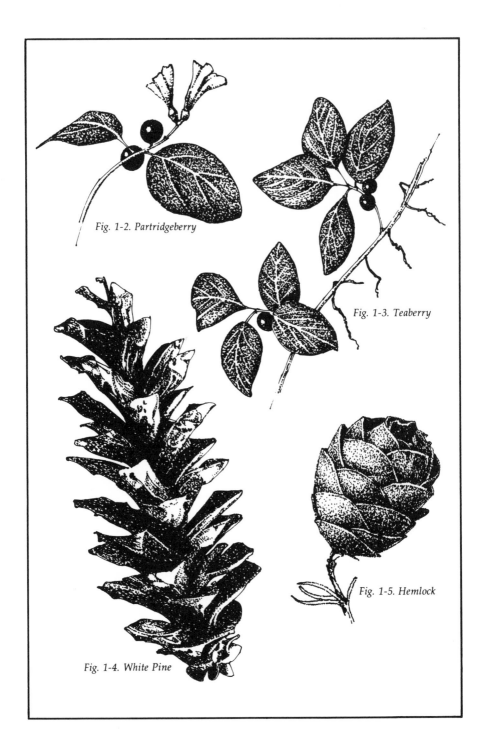

Fig. 1-2. Partridgeberry

Fig. 1-3. Teaberry

Fig. 1-4. White Pine

Fig. 1-5. Hemlock

Fresh greens should also be cut at an angle (never rip them from the tree; use pruning shears) and kept in water until used. (Here again, put freshly cut greens in hot water first, then keep container filled with tap water.) Cut long branches; you can clip them into shorter sprigs as you need them. Plants such as partridge-berry and teaberry should be kept in loosely tied plastic bags and sprinkled with water occasionally to keep them from drying out.

Dried material (cones, pods, etc.) should be stored in paper bags and placed out of the reach of mice and squirrels. If you keep the bags in a shed or barn, hang them. Many people bake seeds and pods in a 300°F. oven for half an hour to be sure they don't harbor insects.

Back from the hike in the woods with your bags and bundles of these natural materials, you can start on the decorations that will embellish your home throughout the holidays.

WREATHS

Fig. 2-1. Spruce cones may be used for a wreath
base, instead of white pine, but they are stiffer
and harder to push into the frame.

THERE is nothing so welcoming as a wreath on a front door, and the tradition is an old one. But every decade seems to bring new media for wreath-making: in addition to the familiar fresh greens or dried herbs, wreaths are now made of straw, cones, woven vines, tissue paper, velvet, patchwork, clay — almost anything.

And they are no longer limited to gracing only the front door. Hang wreaths in the kitchen, on the back door, from candle sconces, or over mantels — or arrange a wreath on a table around the punch bowl.

For the front door, most people still prefer the traditional wreath of dried herbs or fresh greens. Both are surprisingly easy to make, if you use the right materials. The construction process is much the same; both employ a wire device known as a "double wreath frame" (Fig. 2-1). This is a three-dimensional frame in two layers, available inexpensively at florist shops. There are other types of frames, but this particular kind is the easiest to use, especially for the beginner. Commercial wreaths are often wired on a single-layer, crimped-wire ring, but it takes considerable practice to make a nice sturdy wreath using this.

It is nearly impossible to create an attractive wreath from a simple piece of wire or a coat hanger. Since the wire is smooth, the greens have nothing to cling to. No matter how tightly you wire and how hard you pull, the branches will slip and will not surround the wreath fully and evenly. You will end up not only with an awkward-looking, skimpy wreath, but with a good deal of trouble in the bargain.

Once you've made a wreath or two, you may be able to devise your own substitutes for the double frame. (I once used the lid of a big wooden cheese box and I have a friend who managed with a pair of barrel hoops!)

Wrap the frame in extra-wide bias tape, or bias-cut strips of old sheets. It takes a little more work to cut these strips on the bias (diagonally), but it is time well spent, because the fabric will stretch if cut this way. The strips should be about 2 inches wide.

Using one continuous strip (stitch several together for a large wreath), wrap the wreath frame in a solid spiral so no wire is showing. Don't pull it too tight — the fabric should be snug but not stretched. Secure the end with a few firm stitches. You will now have a whole series of evenly spaced pockets into which you will push the stems of whatever plant material you use (Fig. 2-2).

Fig. 2-2. Sprigs of herbs or greens are tucked into pockets formed by successive rows of wrapping.

Green Wreath

For a green wreath, tuck sprigs of white pine, hemlock, balsam, boxwood, cedar, or any green you choose into the pockets. Each type of green is different, but most sprigs work best if about 6 inches in length. Longer sprigs will work on a larger wreath. Each successive row will cover the stems of the previous one. Be sure you fill inner and outer edges, too, so that no fabric shows. If the wreath seems too bushy, use shorter sprigs; if it seems sparse, use longer ones.

You can cover both front and back if you wish, making an even fuller wreath, but remember that it will protrude some distance from your door. I prefer to leave the back flat.

This is your basic wreath and you can decorate it in a number of ways. Sprigs of bittersweet, bayberry, juniper, barberry, holly, or other berries and leaves can be tucked into the pockets between the stems. Pine cones are most easily attached by wiring their stems to florist picks (pointed sticks with thin, strong wire attached to one end) and pushing the pick sticks into the pockets. Or you can wrap fine wire around and under the top layer of "petals" on each cone and tie the ends of the wire through the wreath.

Fresh apples and crab apples are added in the same way, by wiring picks to their stems. Or you can thread a darning needle with the wire and pull it through the fruit. Remember, however, that fresh fruit will not withstand freezing and thawing, so use it only on wreaths that won't be exposed to winter temperatures.

Dried-Herb Wreath

For a dried-herb wreath, use statice or baby's breath or both. A base of statice with sprigs of baby's breath gives an airy, full effect. Handle dried material gently; it is brittle.

You can also use fresh herbal material and let it dry on the wreath. Bay is especially beautiful; lamb's ears (wooly betony), sage, germander, and silver king artemisia are also attractive. These can be mixed, but use a plant with large leaves for the bottom or base layer, adding other plants with smaller leaves on top of this layer, so that the larger leaves do not hide the smaller ones.

This leafy base may be decorated with a variety of dried blossoms — yellow and red *Achillea* (colored varieties of yarrow), straw flowers, lavender spikes, tansy, or nearly any colorful flower. Instead of using them individually, arrange the blossoms in small bunches before adding them to the wreath.

Cone Wreath

Cone wreaths may be constructed in a number of ways. My preference for both ease and durability is to make a glued wreath, but many people prefer to wire each cone in place onto a base layer of large cones. Whether you intend to glue or wire the top cones in place, begin with the same double wreath frame you would use for a fresh wreath, and a supply of cones from the white pine or spruce tree. Wear rubber gloves or old cotton gloves to save your hands from scratches.

To begin a glued wreath, push cones into the space between the top and bottom wire of the frame (Fig.

2-1). The stem ends should be toward the center on a small wreath. On a very large wreath cones can be inserted alternately from the center and the outside of the frame. Most of this layer will be hidden eventually, in any case, by subsequent layers.

Using adhesive caulking glue (which comes in a cylindrical cardboard tube), and with a wide variety of cones, nuts, pods, etc. at hand, begin gluing materials to the cone base. You must use an adhesive rather than a glue that hardens completely, since cones are "live" things that open and close slightly with changes in humidity.

I prefer to complete one area at a time, but many people work around the entire wreath at once. Use the largest cones first, then medium, and finish by using the smallest cones to fill spaces and cover any frame or glue spots that show.

Milkweed pods, horse chestnuts, beechnuts, acorns, sweet-gum pods, and seed heads of wild iris, bergamot, and brown-eyed Susan may also be used on the top layer, along with walnuts, almonds, filberts, brazil nuts, pecans, and butternuts.

Cone wreaths, like those made of dried herbs, will last for many years if stored where mice and squirrels won't find them.

Partridgeberry Wreath

One of the most beautiful and versatile wreaths I've ever seen is made by a friend of mine each Christmas. She begins with a wreath frame small enough to fit inside the rim of a large, round serving plate. (A double wreath frame will work but isn't necessary.) She fills it with damp-ened unshredded sphagnum moss (buy it at any garden shop — or gather your own), then wraps the moss loosely in place with thin wire or invisible thread.

The wreath consists of partridge-berry vines whose roots are tucked firmly into the sphagnum. The bright red berries are striking against the tiny glossy green leaves.

All day this cheerful wreath hangs on Mary's front door. Before supper, she brings it in and places it in the serving plate, which has about ¼ inch of water in it. She sets a bowl of fruit in the center and transforms the wreath into a center-piece; at the same time, it absorbs moisture through the sphagnum — moisture it will retain all through the next day while on the door.

Tissue-Paper Wreath

Other lovely wreaths can be made from materials you won't have to go to the woods to find. Tissue paper makes a beautiful wreath when cut in 8-inch-long, 1-inch-wide strips (cut through the whole package at once). Here's a wreath you *can* use a coat hanger for. Bend a wire coat

Fig. 2-3.

Fig. 2-4. Tissue paper strips transform a coat hanger into a durable indoor wreath (made by Julie Rogers).

hanger into a neat circle and, beginning at the hook, twist the strips of tissue paper onto the wire (Fig. 2-3). Continue around the hanger, pushing the completed twists close together until a fluffy, full wreath is formed (Fig. 2-4).

If you choose green tissue, add a few strips of red every so often to suggest berries. A solid white tissue-paper wreath adorned with a red satin bow is elegant when hung on a Wedgwood blue or dark-colored interior door.

How To Tie Bows

Although traditional herb and cone wreaths do not have bows, most other large wreaths do. Some are of satin ribbon for indoor use, others of stiff cotton calico ribbon. Whatever the material, the bow is the finishing touch that can either ruin or highlight the wreath. And except for very tiny ones, most bows look more elegant with long tails. Instructions follow for tying a variety of bows.

A Single Bow: Tie a double knot around something (a pencil is fine) leaving two long ends of equal length — the wider the ribbon, the longer the ends should be. Roughly

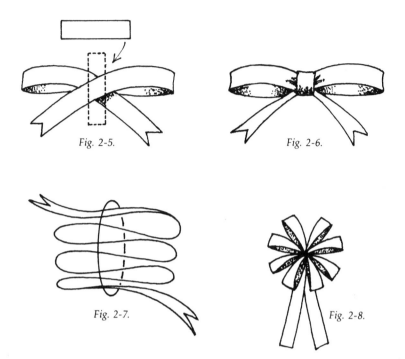

Fig. 2-5.

Fig. 2-6.

Fig. 2-7.

Fig. 2-8.

speaking, each end must be 3 times the width of the finished bow. Add some extra if you want exceptionally long tails on the bow.

Fold the left-hand tail under to make a loop. Bend the loop over across the knot to the right side. Leave your left index finger behind it, between it and the double knot. Your thumb is on top.

Bring the right tail up and over your left thumb and the loop, under your index finger and back through the space that your left thumb is occupying.

With your right index finger, push this loop through until it is big enough to grasp. Hold it and the center band of the bow by closing your right thumb over it. Remove

left hand and use it to grasp the loop, which is now on the left side. Pull the loop through to tighten knot slightly.

Don't pull it crimped-tight yet, since you may want to tighten or loosen it to make the bow even. You can slip the loops and tails in order to make them the size you want.

When you are happy with it, firm the knot by pulling on the *back* of the left-hand loop and the *front* of the right-hand loop. That tightens the knot without disturbing the bow at all.

Slip the knot off the pencil and use the little loop on the back as a base for attaching the bow to your wreath.

A Stitched Bow: Cut a long piece

of ribbon and determine its center. Fold both ends in and past the center, crossing them at the center and forming two loops the size you want your bow (Fig. 2-5). Cut a short piece of ribbon, fold it over the center to form the "knot" and pull it tight enough to puff the bow and make it look tied. Then simply stitch this ribbon loop in the back, stitching through the crossed ribbon, but not through the front of the knot (Fig. 2-6).

A Multi-looped Bow: A way to make a full and less formal bow, perfect for cotton ribbons, is to make a series of loops (like ribbon candy), holding it in the center. Take a long piece of thin, very flexible wire (Fig. 2-7) and wind it tightly about the center. As you wind, the ribbon will gather into folds that make the loops stand out. Then all you have to do is separate the loops slightly (Fig. 2-8), and attach two pieces of ribbon for the tails.

DECKING
THE HALLS

*Fig. 3-1. Colorful fresh fruit can fill a hurricane
globe for an elegant mantel arrangement.*

DECORATING your home for
the Christmas season is a
labor of love. It isn't a project
you have to set about purposefully
one day and complete on the spot.
Like Topsy, it just grows.

Fresh greens appear, an armful at
a time, and gradually take over the
house in ropes and arrangements.
Some dreary day the children can
soap-stencil scenes on their bed-
room windows, and munch on the
freshly popped corn they are stringing into festoons. Boxes and baskets
of ribbon, gift wrap, tags, and

Christmas cards creep in and all at
once are everywhere. A big wooden
bowl of pomanders with sprigs of
pine becomes the centerpiece on the
dining-room table.

Christmas is more fun this way,
little by little, instead of being a
major obstacle to overcome.

Roping

Greens and fresh fruit are nearly
everyone's favorite decorating materials. Roping of fresh evergreens is
lovely, graceful, and versatile, but
many people don't use it because

they don't know how to make it. It does take time, but it is not at all difficult. Cedar or white-pine boughs make good roping because they are soft and flexible.

Begin with a soft rope. Heavy or stiff rope won't drape properly and slippery ones like nylon cord are hard to wire materials to. Soft cotton clothesline cord is perfect. If it is stiff, gather it into a loose skein, and run it through the washing machine once or twice to soften it.

Roping is much easier to make if the clothesline is tightly stretched. Tie one end to a door knob and the other to the leg of a very heavy table and work along it.

Cut greens 4 to 5 inches long and bundle 3 or 4 pieces into a little bouquet. Wrap thin, flexible wire around the stem end of these bundles to hold them firmly together. I like to make a whole basketful of little bunches and then attach them to the rope all at once.

Wire the bundles to the stretched rope so that each bunch covers the stems of the preceding one. Attach them around the rope in a spiral so it is covered on all sides. You can vary the thickness of the roping by using more or fewer bunches per foot of rope.

These ropes are perfect for winding around banisters, pillars, newel posts, lampposts, etc. If the rope is to hang in a swag, however, it is better to measure the bare rope against the area where you plan to use it. Then mark the intersections so the greens will be facing the right way.

For example, if the rope is to be draped over a window, make a pencil mark at the center of the rope and drape it where the completed green

Fig. 3-2.

Fig. 3-3.

rope will hang; also mark the intersections — the corner points at either side where it will be attached (Fig. 3-2).

When you wire the pine bundles to the rope, work from the center marks toward the corners and from the ends to the corners, so the stem ends point toward the corners (Fig. 3-3). This keeps the pine boughs facing downward when the rope is hung and prevents a bare end from showing. The corners can be covered easily with bows or even a bunch of holly or evergreen.

These green ropes can be highlighted by spiraling them with strings of cranberries or popcorn. Cranberries do not last as well as popcorn and should be strung separately to prevent the pink juice from staining the popcorn. Both are easy to string using quilting thread or any heavy-gauge thread and a long, thin needle.

Put the needle through the center of each cranberry, but slightly off center of the popcorn to avoid the hard kernels. The popcorn should be unbuttered and unsalted, of course. Make two batches — one to eat and one to string.

Chains

Remember those red-and-green construction-paper chains we used to make as children? Like us, paper chains have grown up; made in just the same way, but from beautiful gift-wrapping papers or calico and gingham craft ribbon now available, chains are very sophisticated decorations. If you can find reversible gift wrap, so much the better.

Simply cut a large number of strips about ¾ to 1 inch wide and 4 to 5 inches long. The wider they are, the longer they must be to loop properly. Then proceed as before — the method hasn't changed a bit — alternating sides of the paper if you wish, so rings are reversed, and using white glue or rubber cement. Secure the glued ends with a paper clip as you work; they dry in a very few minutes, so you can use the first clip again quite soon.

If the gift wrap you like is not reversible and you don't want a white interior on your chain, simply double the paper. Cut two strips for each ring and hold them back to back with a drop of glue. Then make a ring as above, treating the two strips as one. It takes a minute longer, but you are not limited to the few patterns available in reversible wrap.

More expensive to make, but longer lasting, are chains of cotton craft ribbon (starched cotton fabric). It comes in many widths, in ginghams and calicos of every color.

If you don't mind a little extra work, you can make this ribbon from any small-print fabric — perhaps to match some accessory or feature of the room — by starching the fabric stiffly, ironing it, and cutting it into strips. The starch gives it body and prevents raveling. Glue the ends of each link with a drop of white glue.

You can make bows to decorate your tree or catch your swagged garlands with, using calico ribbon or strips you have made yourself. (See previous chapter.) The starch will give nearly any fabric enough body for a large bow. Use spray starch on more fragile fabrics to avoid soaking them.

Topiary

Although it's a tedious job, you can make a beautiful topiary "tree" for the holidays by covering a round potato with short sprigs of boxwood or germander (Fig. 3-4). It is best to insert the sprigs at an angle so they overlap slightly, and keep the shiny sides up. If the stems are not very strong, make a hole with a toothpick, nail, or some other pointed object first.

Fill a scrubbed clay flowerpot with wet plaster of Paris or any clay material firm enough to hold the tree. Sharpen a length of dowel (which I prefer to stain dark) in a pencil sharpener and push the blunt end into the plaster or clay. Be sure it's straight and centered in the pot.

When the base is firm, carefully push the greens-studded potato onto the pointed end of the dowel. Cover the clay with moss or any other natural material. I usually tie a bow of red satin ribbon around the dowel, close to the potato (Fig. 3-5).

Fig. 3-4.

Fig. 3-5.

Fruit Arrangement

A large hurricane globe can be put to good use at Christmas. Set it on a small plate and carefully fill it with limes, lemons, tangerines, red apples, and walnuts. Ring the base with a small evergreen wreath to hide the plate and balance the arrangement (Fig. 3-1). Replace the fruit about once a week. Lemons don't keep as well as the other fruits, so you might check them a little more frequently.

Soap Stencils

Soap stencils, which used to decorate the windows of every school, are still a nice touch, especially in a child's room. You can make your own stencils on light cardboard by tracing around cookie cutters or drawing simple outlines of a Christmas tree, candy cane (cut out alternate stripes), candle, gingerbread boy, and other symbols of the season.

On a plate, mix white (real) soap flakes and a little water until sticky and apply this over the cut stencil with a wrung-out sponge. Pat it on, don't rub, then lift the stencil off carefully. The pane will look like etched glass. Don't do this stenciling in the bathroom or in a room near the kitchen where the windows tend to steam.

Baskets

Baskets are attractive containers and help control some of the clutter of the season. Use them to hold large bouquets of greens, concealing a bowl or even a small pail of water inside them. Stud small baskets of apples with sprigs of white pine or hemlock to accent a small table and provide ready snacks.

You can use a variety of split baskets to make the purely utilitarian business of Christmas a little less untidy. To avoid the mess and nuisance of retrieving gift-wrapping materials each time they are needed, or instead of just leaving them all about, keep the paper, string, tape, ribbon, tags, pens, and scissors in a huge split basket (Fig. 3-6). It hides all but the tall rolls of paper and looks nice wherever it

Fig. 3-6. A split basket makes a handsome and handy container for rolls of paper, ribbons, tape, and scissors.

lands. It is easy to carry from place to place, and is handy to have within reach.

Gift wrapping is a sociable activity that may take place anywhere, any time. Sitting by the fire in the evening is a fine time to wrap out-of-household gifts, or boxed and unrecognizable gifts for family members.

Wrapped gifts-to-go can get lost under the tree and are never where you can find them when it's time to deliver them. Stacked neatly in a box or a picnic hamper, they add a decorative touch to your home's entrance area. And, as holiday guests leave, their gifts are handy.

Christmas cards to send, along with stamps, stationery, pens, and address book can stay in a small covered pie basket near your favorite chair. A small pouch-shaped basket can hold the Christmas cards you have received, where everyone can enjoy them (and where they are at hand in case you need a special picture to cut out for decorating a package).

Christmas Cards

Many people tape their cards around a doorway in an informal room. Another attractive way to frame a door with cards is to cut two ribbons the length of the door frame and staple or tack the ribbons to the top edge of the frame where the fastener won't show. As cards arrive, attach them to the ribbon with straight pins.

Even the "business" of Christmas, such as cards and wrapping supplies, can serve as decorations along with the pine boughs and popcorn!

NATIVITY SCENES

Fig. 4-1. Arms for cornhusk crèche figures may be braided instead of rolled to add variety to figures.

THE custom of commemorating the night in Bethlehem with a manger scene or crèche has its origin in the early thirteenth century. St. Francis of Assisi assembled the original *presepio* scene using real people and animals. The idea took root, and before long, several other countries had firmly established traditions of depicting the Nativity with products of their native crafts.

Clay, wood, paper, fabric, metal — almost any medium from which human figures may be formed — can be adapted to a Nativity scene, and nearly every material has been used at one time. In the southern highlands, the cornhusk doll, whose roots are deep in American history, has been used often in beautifully simple manger scenes.

Cornhusk Figures

Cornhusks are a versatile material to work with; when properly dried and then soaked in water, they are strong, flexible, and surprisingly durable. The basic method of making a cornhusk doll can be varied to form and clothe a variety of figures. The size of your figures will depend on the size of the husks. Field corn will allow you to make the largest figures; table corn yields smaller husks.

The husks to use are the fine-textured inside ones, close to the kernels. Discard the tough outer husks with the little "flags" on the end and save only the tapered inner ones (reserve the corn silk for later use). To remove the husks without tearing them, cut off the stem of the ear close to the bottom of the cob and unwrap the husks instead of peeling them back.

Place the husks in a single layer on a screen or rack and lay them in the sun for a day or so until they are thoroughly dry and creamy white. At this point they may be stored indefinitely. (Don't try to work with fresh husks that have not been dried, since they will curl and distort as they dry, ruining your work.)

When you are ready to use the husks, put them in a shallow baking pan or bowl filled with warm water. Wait about five minutes for them to soften before you begin work, and leave each husk in the water until you need it. As you remove a husk, cut off the puckered bottom from the wide end so that it will lie flat (Fig. 4-2).

Stack six or seven long, straight husks of similar size and, using white cotton sewing thread, tie them tightly into a bundle at the pointed ends (Fig. 4-3). Fold the points over, wrap another small husk around them (Fig. 4-4), and secure with thread.

Hold this wrapped end toward you, with the wide ends of the husks pointing up. One by one, fold the long husks down over the wrapped area, pulling each one tight. Pull the last husk down and spread it around the others from side to side, stretching it slightly to form a smooth face. Pull out any wrinkles at the "chin" and tie all the husks securely to form a neck.

Place two long, straight husks on top of each other with their ends reversed (Fig. 4-5) and roll them tightly lengthwise into a pencil-shaped stick. Tie at each end. Divide the body of the doll into two nearly equal parts — one for the front (the side with the smooth face) and one for the back. Split the husks if necessary. Place your pencil-shaped roll between these two sections and push up close to the neck. Tie below the arms to form the waist (Fig. 4-6).

Wrap a husk from the front left side of the waist over the right shoulder and down to the back left side. Hold it there and repeat on the right side using another husk. Tie again at the waist (Fig. 4-7).

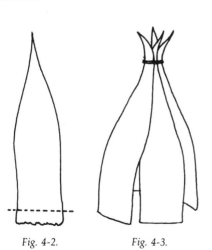

Fig. 4-2.   Fig. 4-3.

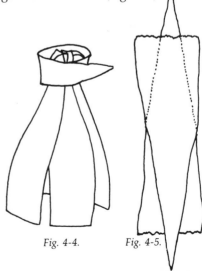

Fig. 4-4.   Fig. 4-5.

Fig. 4-6.   Fig. 4-7.   Fig. 4-8.

Fortunately, the clothing of that time was similar for men and women, so the shepherds, kings or wise men, and Joseph all may be dressed in flowing garments, which obviates the need for legs. Although you can make legs, skirted figures will stand up much better.

For a skirted figure, tie two large, perfect husks, pointed ends down, to the waist of the doll — one in front, one in back. The wide ends should be over the doll's head (Fig. 4-8). Then fold these down over the skirt of the doll to form an overskirt, and secure by tying loosely with thread. These threads can be removed when the doll is dry.

Fold the doll's arms to a desired or appropriate position. The wise men or king figures should have their arms held together in front of them so they can hold gifts; simply tie together the tails of the threads at their wrists. These can be cut off when the doll is dry.

Mary's arms should reach downward; the shepherd needs one arm outstretched for his staff. Tie these in place with threads. Your figures will appear to have been caught in a giant spider's web, but when they are thoroughly dry, these retaining threads can all be cut away. Only the neck and waist threads will remain.

Mary will need a covering for her head. Cut off the pointed end of a large husk and fold the husk like a shawl over her head and shoulders. Tie it in place around her by wrapping it loosely, two or three times, with thread. The threads should not be so tight as to make creases. When the husk/shawl is dry, you will probably want to hold it in place with a drop of white glue.

The wise men or kings will need crowns; cut these from a strip of husk (Fig. 4-9). Tie each crown in place until it is dry and then glue it (glue won't adhere to a wet husk). Also put husk robes around the kings' shoulders. The gifts they hold can be made of a small strip of husk rolled or folded into package-like shapes.

Each shepherd's staff can be made by rolling a long strip of husk and tying it with a spiral of thread. Bend

Fig. 4-9.

Fig. 4-10.

the top into a crook and secure it with thread (Fig. 4-10). When the staff is dry, cut the thread and add a drop of glue if the husk starts to unroll. Drop a bit of glue on the shepherd's hand to hold the staff in place.

For the Child, make a very small doll, going only as far as tying the neck. Wrap the rest of the figure in a folded husk so that only the head shows. Halos can be tiny braids of ⅛-inch strips of husk, or they can be rings formed from a single strip. For hair and beards use corn silk or a natural-colored wool yarn, unraveled. Glue these to the doll when it is thoroughly dried. (Usually, cornhusk dolls will dry overnight, but in hot, humid weather thorough drying may take three to four days.)

Fig. 4-11. Cornhusk dolls may be made in miniature for Christmas tree ornaments (made by Amy and Jim Gibbons).

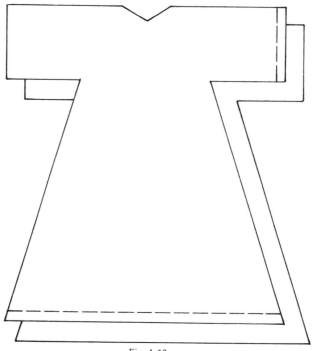

Fig. 4-12.

Clothespin Figures

A more colorful crèche can be made of clothespin dolls. Since fabric is used to dress these figures, there is a great deal of variety possible. The kings' robes can be rich satins and velvets, or all can be dressed in simple cotton fabrics, depending on your taste and the contents of your scrap basket.

The basic dolls are made as shown on p. 48, with their feet glued to buttons. Instead of dressing them in gathered skirt dresses, they should be in simple straight garments (see pattern, Fig. 4-12), with head coverings, robes, and capes varying according to the roles of the dolls.

To make a shepherd's headgear, use a bone ring (the kind used on potholders) painted to match his cloak. Glue or stitch the top of his headgear to the ring (Fig. 4-13). These make good halos, too, when dipped in gold paint or wound with fine gold cord. A staff can be made of wire.

Since wooden clothespins are all one size, the Holy Child will have to be made of a small wooden bead stitched to a bundle of fabric. Cut a 2-inch circle of fabric and gather it around the edge. Fill loosely with a cotton ball and pull the gathering thread to form a bundle. As demonstrated in Fig. 4-14, push a needle through the fabric bundle and then through the small wooden bead. Put a small tuft of hair-colored yarn over the top of the hole and push the needle back through the bead (with

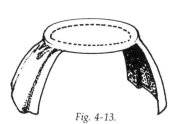

Fig. 4-13.

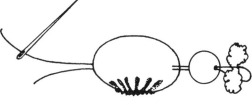

Fig. 4-14.

the thread around the yarn) and the bundle. Pull taut enough to secure the "hair," and pull the bead head into the fabric to suggest a wrapped baby. Tie the thread and glue the baby into half a walnut shell. Glue the hair down over the bead if necessary.

If you wish to give variety to the height of the figures by showing a kneeling Mary, simply saw the clothespin off about 1½ inches from the bottom and glue it to the button base. Arrange Mary's dress so it folds under the button and gives the appearance of a kneeling figure.

Stiff fabrics are desirable when making clothespin figures for doll houses or other similar uses because they give body to the dresses. But for the Nativity costumes, softer, draped lines are better. Thin knits, well-washed sheer fabrics, and the very thin silks used to make inexpensive square neck scarves are perfect. So are many fabrics that have been washed over and over again, such as handkerchieves and children's clothes. However you choose to dress your clothespin Nativity figures, they, like the cornhusk crèche, will be uniquely your own.

If you find the crèche to be more work than you care to do, any of these figures can be used as Christmas tree ornaments simply by attaching a hanger of thread or ribbon to each one (Figs. 4-1 and 4-11).

SMALL GIFTS TO MAKE

Fig. 5-1. "Nine-patch" (left) and "Pine Tree State" (right) are good quilt patterns for balsam pillows.

THE handmade gift requires time and planning, and therefore it says you care enough to give something of yourself.

Balsam Sachet and Pillow

Few gifts require as much planning as balsam pillows and sachets if you want to make them with the needles of last year's Christmas tree! As soon as the ornaments are safely boxed and carried to the attic, you can begin stripping the tree of its needles. Once gathered, they last indefinitely. We store them in brown paper bags.

This is not to say you can't use fresh balsam needles — they work just fine. What *is* essential is that the needles are balsam. Other evergreen needles have only a faint smell of pitch, a far cry from the familiar balsam scent, and will not do. To my knowledge, there's no place to buy needles, so you must collect them from the tree itself.

The simplest balsam sachet is a 2½x5-inch cloth bag, hemmed at the top, firmly stuffed with needles, and tied with a narrow-ribbon bow. Because balsam cones are large, use two hemlock cones instead to decorate the bow, attaching them with thread.

The scent from a balsam pillow can fill an entire room in humid weather. The pillow can be plain or fancy, but it is best to keep it fairly small (no larger than 10 inches).

Nearly any simple quilt block design done in green and white is appropriate — a nine patch can be pieced in any size on the sewing machine. (A nine patch is just that: nine squares all the same size, assembled in three rows to form a square [Fig. 5-1, left].)

A little more work but beautiful is a "Pine Tree State" block done in green on an 8-inch-square white background (Fig. 5-1, right). It can be pieced, but appliqué is easier and the effect is much the same. For this design, cut out each piece (A., B., C., D., and E.) according to the patterns in Fig. 5-2. Assemble the six main ones (A., B., and C.) and stitch them together. Press all the edges under. Add the trunk (D.) and base (E.), with edges pressed under. Center the tree diagonally on a square of white Indianhead or other firm fabric and hand appliqué in place. Stitch to a solid green backing (right sides together), leaving one side open, and turn.

Make a separate pillow of two squares of firm muslin ½ inch smaller all around than the pillow cover. Fill with balsam, stitch to close, put inside the finished pillow top, and stitch to close. This way no sharp little needles will stick out through the seams, and the cover can be removed for washing.

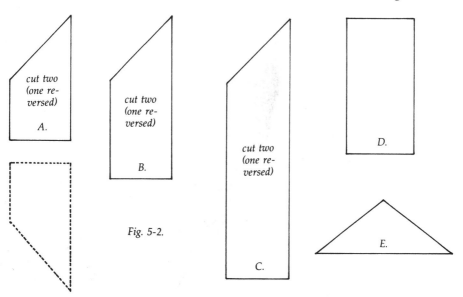

Fig. 5-2.

Christmas Potpourri

Balsam is also the basis of a special Christmas potpourri blend. This is a pretty combination that smells and looks like the season (Fig. 5-3). Mix 1 cup dry balsam needles with 1 cup balsam or hemlock tips (about 2 inches of twig and needles), 1 cup hemlock cones, 1 cup dried red rose petals, 1 cup dried orange peel in pieces as big as 1 inch, 1 cup stick cinnamon broken into 1- or 2-inch pieces, ¼ cup whole cloves, ½ cup bay leaves, ½ cup dried calendula blossoms, ½ cup other mixed dried blossoms, ¼ cup dried rosemary, ½ cup dried fragrant rosebuds and petals, and up to 1 cup of other dried herbs and mild-scented blossoms, such as lemon verbena, peppermint, spearmint, marjoram (*not* lavender), and up to 1 cup of other spices and dried citrus peels such as whole allspice, star anise, lemon, and grapefruit. (Use only ¼ cup each of the spices.) Add 2 tablespoons orris root chips mixed with 6 drops of oil of rose to preserve the rose scent, and mix well.

This is strong enough to leave uncovered for the holidays in a basket, bowl, or box, where it looks as pretty as it smells. Add colorful accents like bittersweet and holly berries as they fall from other decorations, if you wish. You might want to keep a wooden cheese box filled with this mixture in the kitchen, and scoop out a little into a striped paper bag as each guest departs. If you omit the cones and the balsam or hemlock tips, you can use the potpourri to fill sachets.

Lavender Bag

Lavender bags are fun to make and can be presented separately or

Fig. 5-3. A hand-painted antique blueberry box is the perfect container for Christmas potpourri (box by Jan Krise).

Fig. 5-4. A lace-edged lavender bag will keep a whole closet full of linens delicately scented.

in sets for a larger gift. For each, you will need a 7-inch circle of lavender-colored gingham or calico, 10 inches of ¼-inch lavender or cream-colored satin ribbon, 23 inches of tatted-type lace, and a scant ¼ cup of dried French lavender.

Stitch lace around the edge of the fabric circle, turning under a very narrow single hem as you stitch. (This may be done by hand or on the sewing machine.) The lace should cover the raw edge on the inside.

Place lavender in the center of the fabric and gather edges upward to form a ball. Tie securely with ribbon into a neat bow, trimming both ends to the same length. Pull the edges of the fabric outward to firm the lavender and flare the ruffle (Fig. 5-4).

Spice Rope

Spice ropes were used to freshen kitchen air long ago, and have recently enjoyed a revival. They are simply small sachets full of kitchen spices (whole cloves, broken stick cinnamon, whole allspice) and dried orange peel, tied to a braid of matching yarn (Fig. 5-5).

The sachets are made like the lavender bag, but instead of hemming the edges with lace, cut the circles with pinking shears. Tie with yarn or ribbon.

Cut five 30-inch lengths of knitting worsted from each of three colors, or fifteen strips of one color. Put them through a 1-inch gold or bone ring and fold them so the ends meet and the ring is in the middle. You will have 30 strands; divide them into three groups of ten and braid them. Tie ends with yarn or ribbon.

Space the sachets along the braid and secure them with a few wraps of matching sewing thread. Push a cinnamon stick through the braid near the ring. While spice ropes are nice all through the year, they are especially pretty made with red, green, and white materials and used as Christmas decorations.

Tea Cosy

My mother always claimed that tea cosies went out of style with hoops and bustles, until she made one as a gift and everybody else started asking her for one. With homes colder today, they are definitely back in fashion! A very simple one can be made from the pre-quilted fabrics now available in ginghams and a variety of prints (Fig. 5-7).

Cut four pieces of quilted fabric and two pieces of quilt batting according to the pattern in Fig. 5-6. (Quilt batting is sold in nearly all fabric stores and departments, and gives your cosy extra bulk and insulation.)

Baste gathered eyelet lace (it takes about ¾ yard) to the right side of the fabric around the rounded edge of one piece, with the lace facing *in* and the raw edges of the lace and fabric together. Pin the lace at the corners so it won't be caught in the machine stitching. Cover lace with a second piece of the quilted fabric, right sides together. Stitch edges, using a narrow seam. Turn and remove pins from corners.

Pin two remaining quilted-fabric pieces, right sides together, and put a plain piece of batting over each side, so batting is on the outside. Stitch rounded edge through all four layers, deepening seam as you near the rounded corners and narrowing it as you return to the base

Fig. 5-5. Spice sachets in holiday fabrics are tied on a braid of red, white, and green yarn to make a spice rope (made by Joan Keenan Farrel).

of the side seam. Trim seam.

Turn ruffle-edged piece inside out and lining right side out. Put lining inside ruffle-edged piece (right sides will be together) and pin bottom edges together. Stitch bottoms together, leaving an 8-inch space. Turn to right side and blind stitch the opening. Stitch a bone ring (the kind used on potholders — look for them at any notions counter) to the center of the top.

For an even more special gift, mix ¼ pound of loose black tea with a 3-inch cinnamon stick broken up and the dried peel of one orange, cut small. (To dry the orange peel, cut it in narrow strips and spread it in a pie tin. Placed on a radiator or the shelf of a wood cook stove, the orange peel will dry overnight. In a

Fig. 5-6.

250°F. oven, it takes half an hour and smells divine.) Package the mixture in a plastic bag and tie with a ribbon that matches the tea cosy. Put a ribbon through the bone ring and tie the two together with a bow.

Potholders

If you think potholders are a prosaic gift, try to buy them at a craft show! A set of three matching potholders is hardly an inexpensive stocking stuffer! But it is a welcome offering for any kitchen, especially if the potholders are beautiful, washable, and thickly padded (Fig. 5-8).

Before you begin to think about what the outside of the potholder will look like, consider the inside. The most beautiful holder in the world stuffed with synthetic fiber quilt batting is useless for protecting your hand from heat. You may add an extra layer to make the potholder look fuller, but the business part of the stuffing should be thick cotton so it holds back the heat of the pan. Several layers of terry-cloth towel or a section of old mattress pad gives the best insulation.

The outside fabric should be washable and flexible, a cotton or cotton blend. (Synthetics melt at too low a temperature.) And the size should be ample.

Now that you know all my pre-

Fig. 5-7. A padded tea cosy is easily made from pre-quilted fabric (made by Dee Radcliffe).

Fig. 5-8. Potholders may actually be pieced as you would a quilt block, or made from printed fabrics that simulate quilt patterns (made by Dee Radcliffe).

judices about potholders, you may proceed! Quilt blocks are a natural for potholders, but unless they are simple enough to be done on a sewing machine, they are a lot of work for something that is bound to get blueberry pie all over it. A classic nine-patch square (see balsam pillows, pp. 32-33) is easy, as are some of the appliquéd ones that can be adapted to machine appliqué. And there is nothing wrong with a potholder made of plain fabric, especially in a pretty print.

Use a firm fabric as a base and as backing — not only because of its strength, but because it's easier to appliqué to. Stick to simple designs with few sharp corners, unless you are very good at machine appliqué. Be daring in your fabric combinations, mixing ginghams, stripes, prints, and solids. The potholder itself can be a fancy shape as long as

it is a practical one to make and to use. A pig, owl, and apple are all good basic shapes, and you can embroider or machine appliqué the details, such as face or leaves, to one side.

Once you have the front completed, cut a matching back. Round the corners slightly to make binding easier and machine stitch one edge of bias binding to the front piece. Make a sandwich of front, filling, and back (with right sides out — just as the finished potholder will look), and pin binding over all to back. Blind stitch the binding into place, catching all layers occasionally to secure the filling. Stitch a ring to one corner. You can use a loop of bias tape, but a ring is much easier to hang since it stays round.

To present, stack a set of three matching or coordinated potholders and tie with a crossed ribbon.

Fig. 5-9. A round towel with a cord for tying at the center is always handy when needed (made by Shirley Radcliffe).

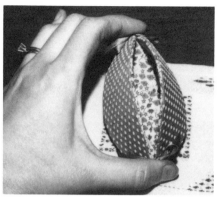

Fig. 5-11. A pinch box opens when the ends are squeezed together and closes when released (made by Julie Rogers).

Kitchen Towel

A very simple and very useful gift is a set of towels that tie to the refrigerator door or to a handy drawer pull near the sink (Fig. 5-9). Cut two circles as big as you can fit on a large bath towel and bind the edges of the circles with matching bias tape. (Save the leftover corners of the towels to use as stuffing for potholders.) In the very center of the circles, stitch the middle of a long piece of bias tape (12 to 18 inches), which has been folded lengthwise and stitched to form a stout cord (Fig. 5-10). The cord can be tied to a hook, drawer pull, or refrigerator door where the towel will always be handy!

Pinchbox

One of the prettiest little containers ever made is the old-fashioned pinchbox, an elliptical, three-sided box that opens when the ends are pinched together. I have one of Victorian ancestry done in old silks, but I understand they are even older in origin. From thimble size to 5 inches long, and covered in whatever fabric was at hand, they were used to hold anything from

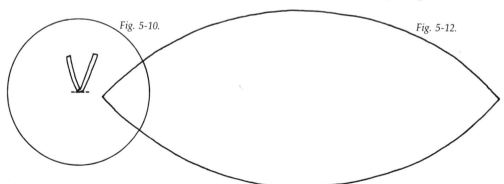

Fig. 5-10.

Fig. 5-12.

sewing accessories and tatting to small treasures. Mine came to me as the cradle for a tiny China doll that had been the prized possession of several generations of little girls before me. Construction couldn't be simpler.

Cut six ellipses (see pattern, Fig. 5-12) out of thin, flexible cardboard, about the weight of a calling card or a manilla folder. Cut 6 pieces of fabric ¼ inch larger all around than the cardboard. Press edges of fabric over cardboard pieces and catch with a zigzag of thread back and forth on the wrong side just to hold in place. Necktie silk, thin calico, and gingham are perfect, as is any thin, soft fabric.

The ellipses can be all the same, in two sets of three, all different, or as mine is — three different pieces for the outside but all three inside pieces the same. Put the three sets together in pairs, wrong sides facing, and secure with white glue. Press under a stack of books or other weight until dry. Glue the ends of a small loop of narrow ribbon into the point of one pair of ellipses if you wish to hang the box.

Join the three double-sided ellipses along the edges with tiny overcast stitches, leaving one of the paired edges completely open. When the two ends of the completed box are pinched together, this side opens (Fig. 5-11). When the pinch is released, it closes.

Depending on the fabric, you may want to embroider the edges with fine blanket or feather stitching. (See Fig. 5-15 for diagrams of stitches.) Mine has no loop, but has tiny satin-ribbon bows stitched at both ends.

Although a pinchbox is a fine gift when empty, its possibilities for fill-ing are limitless. For a little girl it might hold a tiny doll, as mine did, or wrapped candies; for a lady, a sewing kit with embroidery scissors or a packet of a favorite tea or soap.

Other Victorian whimseys that make thoughtful and attractive gifts include needlebooks, pincushions, and handmade cases for scissors or eyeglasses.

The same principle of covered cardboard used to make the pinchbox is the basis of needlebooks and scissors cases, still useful accessories for a sewing basket.

Needlebook

A needlebook is made of two pieces of firm cardboard (shirt cardboard or the backs of scratch pads) cut 3x4 inches. Cut a piece of satin, silk, or other fancy fabric 6x8 inches, and another piece of thin fabric 4½x7 inches. Place the satin face down and lay the two cardboard pieces on it, leaving ¼ to ½ inch of satin showing between them so the book will fold.

Turn the edges over the cardboard and press to hold them down. Miter the corners if necessary. Press the second smaller fabric piece so the edges are turned under, leaving it just smaller than the cardboard. Lay it face up on the satin-covered cardboard and blind stitch it in place to form a lining.

Cut two pieces of very fine wool (or wool blend) flannel 3½x5 inches, using pinking shears. Lay these on top of the lining, centering them, and stitch them through the binding of the book, in the center (Fig. 5-13). Fold the book closed and make a few stitches through the folded binding to encourage it to stay folded (Fig. 5-14). If it won't, hold it over steam

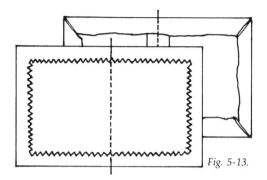

Fig. 5-13.

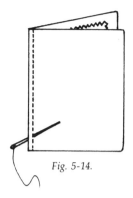

Fig. 5-14.

from a teakettle for a minute and press it under a heavy book.

To decorate the front, cut a design from a piece of lace or use a strip to frame the edge of the cover and blind stitch it in place. If you have a piece of old lace or tatting, you can adapt the size and shape of the book to fit the dimensions of the lace or tatting.

Scissors Case

Scissors cases and eyeglasses cases are similarly constructed. For these, you cover and line two pieces of cardboard separately, then stitch the pieces together. The size and shape of the scissors case will depend on the scissors it is to hold. A tear-drop shape is easy to adapt to fit anything

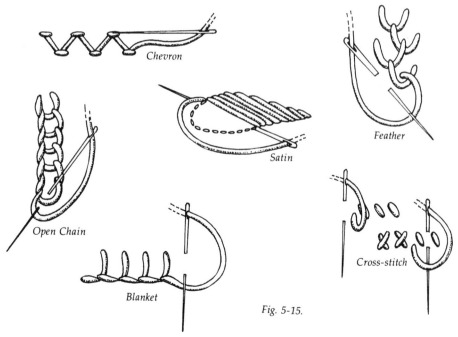

Chevron

Feather

Satin

Open Chain

Cross-stitch

Blanket

Fig. 5-15.

Fig. 5-16. A scissors case (left) and pincushion (right) are handy accessories for a sewing room. (Scissors case by Tillie Sobieski.)

from embroidery scissors to dress-makers' shears. The back piece is large enough to cover the scissors and the front piece is cut off so the handles are exposed (Fig. 5-16, left).

After covering and lining both pieces, stitch them together with a whipstitch. Each edge is then covered with a row of embroidery stitches: chevron, open-chain, feather, or blanket stitches work well. For a Victorian look, use silk (or rayon) embroidery floss.

If you don't have a piece of lace to decorate with, you can use a printed fabric, such as necktie silk, or a bro-cade. The latter is best for large cases; small cases are easier to decorate in a thinner fabric. Or you can embroider a design on the out-side fabric before you use it to cover the cardboard.

For a more elegant effect, both sides of the cardboard were often padded with single layers of soft flannel before covering with fabric. The fabric for the lining should be smooth and tightly woven so the scissors points won't catch on it.

Eyeglasses Case

A particularly nice gift for some-one who wears glasses is a set of spectacles cases to match various outfits — from elegant satin and lace to sporty calico or gingham. The case is made the same way as a scissors case, except you cut out rec-tangular shapes (approximately 3½x6 inches) with rounded corners. Remember to use a soft fabric for the lining and a layer of padding, since many modern-day spectacles have plastic lenses!

Pincushions

Pincushions can be stuffed with any one of a number of fillings, from sawdust to worn-out nylon stockings. The best filling is raw lamb's wool, since pins penetrate it easily and its natural oils keep the pins lubricated and protected from rust. Polyfiber filling is a good substitute, although it does not have the oil. Don't use cotton batting, since it will mat and pins won't slide easily. Also, pins tend to rust more easily in cotton.

Sewing Circle: A "sewing circle" is a very handy accessory to keep on the bureau or hang in a convenient place for quick repairs. It is a large pincushion surrounded by pockets that hold spools of thread (Fig. 5-17).

Cut two 11-inch circles of cotton fabric. They can be alike, or one can be print and the other solid. Stitch gathered eyelet or narrow lace around the edge of one circle, turning under a very narrow single hem as you stitch. (If one fabric is print, put the lace on *it*.) Stitch bias tape around the edge of the other circle. Pin them together, right sides out.

Measure in 2 inches from the edge and stitch the two circles together, stitching a circle inside the original one but leaving about a 3-inch opening for inserting the stuffing. At 2½- to 3-inch intervals, stitch radiating lines starting ¼ inch from the stitched circle toward the outer edge (Fig. 5-18).

Stuff center tightly with lamb's wool or polyfiber and close the opening. Cut 1 yard of ¼-inch ribbon, attach a small safety pin on one end, and thread it through the little space between the radiating lines and the stitched circle and through the center of a small spool of thread. Continue around. One spool should be in each pocket. Tie the ribbon in a bow and clip the ends at an angle. Put a few pins and needles in the cushion to present. The spool stays

Fig. 5-17. A sewing circle keeps needles, pins, and a variety of threads handy for quick mending jobs. (Design by Emma Rutherig.)

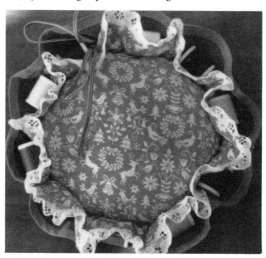

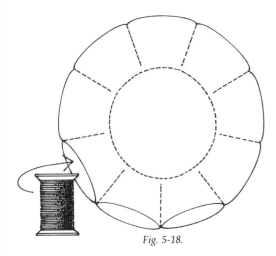

Fig. 5-18.

right on the ribbon when a length of thread is pulled from it.

More conventional pincushions are less complicated to make, but are elegant gifts. They can be made in sizes ranging from tiny ones for tying on the sewing machine to the larger, dressing-table pincushions. Try using the patterns for the satin fruit Christmas tree ornaments (see pp. 74-76), but make them in velvet or velveteen. Enlarge the strawberry pattern so that the straight sides are 4 or 5 inches long.

Sewing Machine Pincushion: For a handy pincushion that hangs on the sewing machine, simply fold a 3½-inch length of 1½-inch-wide ribbon (satin, moiré, grosgrain, or even fancy embroidered) in half crosswise, right sides together. Stitch cut end and one side, turn, and stuff. Make a loop of a 2½-inch length of matching ¼-inch ribbon and pin it to the center of the open side, with its tails inside. Use tiny whipstitches to close the remaining

side, stitching the loop in position as you sew.

Dressing-Table Pincushion: Larger, dressing-table cushions can be made of two matching rectangles of sturdy fabric, such as linen or velvet. These should be about 4½x6½ inches. Embroider a design on the center of one — a simple cross-stitch looks good on linen, and a floral design done in silk or rayon floss is appropriate for velvet.

Place rectangles with right sides facing and stitch together, leaving a space in the center of one long side. Turn, stuff, and close with tiny whipstitches. You can cover the seam with a row of cross-stitches or feather stitches, whichever is appropriate, in the same color as the top embroidery if you wish.

Puffed Pincushion: For a puffed pincushion, use a fancy napkin ring — metal or wood — and cut a circle of velvet twice its diameter. Gather the edge and stuff velvet circle tightly so it will fit into the napkin ring and stand up in a puff. Secure with white glue and cover bottom with a circle of leather or felt glued in place (Fig. 5-16, right).

This is just a sampling of the many attractive small gifts you can make — add your own creative touches by combining patterns and ideas, varying fabrics, and tailoring designs to suit the tastes and interests of the people who will receive the gifts. There's only one feeling nicer than receiving a gift that has been made just for you, in your favorite color, style, or design — and that is giving one.

TOYS TO MAKE

Fig. 6-1. Clothespin dolls may have yarn hair or painted hair with a button for a topknot (made by Tillie Sobieski).

C HRISTMAS is too often characterized by a huge pile of toys. But it has not always been so. There were times when only a very few well-chosen, carefully made toys were to be found on Christmas morning. These were cherished and cared for and lasted for years. Almost every attic still has one or two such toys tucked away somewhere. They were simple toys that required some imagination, some thought, some activity from the child. And we can learn a lot and take good counsel from them.

The dolls didn't talk, walk, sing, or eat real food. They were usually soft, lovable, and durable, and most were made of what was on hand.

Stocking Dolls

Stockings have been a popular material for dolls almost since the first pair came off the knitting needles. When commercially knit socks and stockings became available, stocking dolls were right behind them. They are simple to make, practical, and cuddly — all three characteristics quite opposite to those of most modern "store-bought" dolls.

They are usually made of men's socks, but any size sock will work. Use short cotton socks in either black, brown, or white. Men's cotton socks don't come in pink — you'll have to make a smaller doll from a child's sock if you want pink skin. Black or brown dolls stay

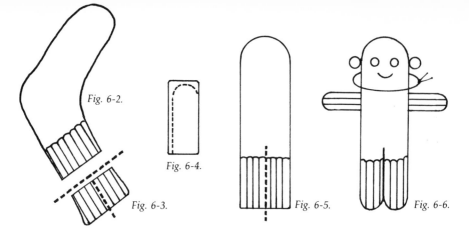

Fig. 6-2.

Fig. 6-4.

Fig. 6-3.

Fig. 6-5.

Fig. 6-6.

cleaner longer — white ones sometimes look within a week as though they'd been used as dustmops!

Fold the top of the sock over so the top edge meets the beginning of the ribbing above the heel, a little above the shoe top (Fig. 6-2). Cut the stocking along the fold so you have half the sock top separate from the rest, and cut that piece in two lengthwise (Fig. 6-3). Stitch each piece down the open side and across one end (Fig. 6-4). Turn and stuff with cotton batting, fiber filling, or old nylon stockings, which will make the doll washable. These are the doll's arms. Set aside.

Flatten the sock so that the heel is underneath instead of on one side and cut lengthwise to the top of the ribbing to form legs (Fig. 6-5). Methods vary from this point. I find

it easiest to cut a 3- to 4-inch slit up the very center of the sole of the foot, which will become the back of the doll, and turn and stuff through that.

Turn the stocking inside out and stitch around the feet and up the leg inseams to close completely. Turn by pulling legs and head through the slit in the back.

Stuff the doll, beginning with the head, and tie it firmly at the neck with matching thread (Fig. 6-6). Make the head a little larger in proportion to the rest of the doll.

Some people prefer to embroider the face before stuffing, using a darning egg as a base, but I find it hard to judge just how the face should be placed on an empty stocking. After the face is stuffed, the positions of the eyes and mouth

Fig. 6-7.

Fig. 6-8.

Fig. 6-9.

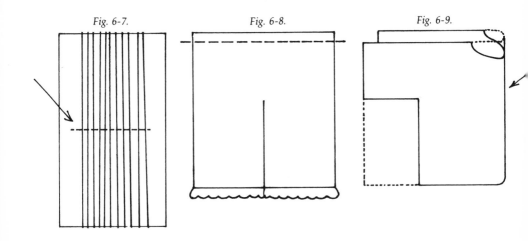

Fig. 6-10.

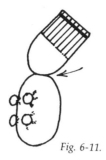

Fig. 6-11.

Fig. 6-12.

suggest themselves. Use double-strand embroidery floss and hide the knots by pulling the needle through the top or back of the head.

Stuff the legs and body and close the slit with overcast stitches. Stitch the arms in place with overcast stitches. Make hair from yarn. Short, curly hair is formed by making a lot of short yarn loops all around the head. Pigtails are made by winding the yarn around a shirt cardboard (the length of it) and stitching right through the cardboard across the center (Fig. 6-7). Cut ends and rip the cardboard away from the stitching. Sew the "part" to the center of the doll's head, pull hair together at the ears, tack, and braid. Tie with ribbons.

All that remains is to dress the doll. For ankle-length bloomers or pantalets, draw a pattern around the legs and allow an extra inch each

way. Remember to make them extra long at the top to accommodate the generous bottom formed by the heel of the sock. Cut pantalets from fabric, stitch (right sides together), turn, gather waist, and add lace at the ankles (Fig. 6-8).

Make a blouse pattern to fit in the same way, allowing the extra inch all around except at the neck (Fig. 6-9), and cut blouse from fabric. Cut down center *back* fold. Assemble by stitching arm and side seams of blouse, binding neck and sleeves with bias tape or gathered lace edging. For now, leave center back edges raw.

Make a skirt from a rectangle of matching fabric; its short side will be the length of the skirt, and should be 1 inch longer than the finished skirt to allow for the hem. Gather skirt and stitch back seam, leaving a 2-inch seam opening in the top to correspond to the open back seam of the blouse. Hem the skirt. Stitch blouse tail to gathered skirt waist, with skirt seam in center back. Bind edge of entire back opening with bias tape, and close with two tiny snaps, one at the neck and one at the waist.

A bandana, apron, earrings, even felt shoes can be added as you wish.

Much simpler are the stocking babies made from white or pastel baby socks with colored bands or

Fig. 6-13. Baby socks make tiny stocking dolls.

lace at the ankle. With this doll, the sock is used so that the toe is the baby's bottom and the heel is the face.

Stuff a baby sock with cotton, forming four little balls either all in front or at the sides. If you do them all in front, it will look like a roller-skate at this stage (Fig. 6-10). Tie these firmly with thread and pull the ends inside with a needle. You can continue from one ball to the other with the same needle and thread. Take a tiny stitch for a tummy button, and pull it tight to form a dent.

Continue to stuff, tying the neck just below the heel of the sock (Fig. 6-11). While the sock is still open, embroider a face of three tiny stitches. Tie the top of the head and fold the stocking over to form a hat. Pull the hat back and make 3 or 4 stitches to form a little fringe of hair (Fig. 6-12). Pull the hat back down but let part of the hair show below it. You can add a pompom at the crown of the hat if you wish, or turn up a brim on the hat (Fig. 6-13).

Clothespin Dolls

For older children with doll houses, a clothespin doll is the perfect size for 1/12-scale doll furnishings. These dolls date from the nineteenth century and were popular even among children without doll houses. A child could have a number of dolls the same size and use them as characters in endless stories and games (Fig. 6-1).

The early clothespins were flat on the sides, so the earliest dolls have faces painted onto one flat side. Later dolls were made with round-topped pins and are even more realistic. If you can't find clothespins

with good round heads (some have only a flat pad on top), glue wooden beads to the tops for heads.

There are several ways of making arms. The most common is to wrap a pipe cleaner once around the doll at the shoulders (Fig. 6-14), leaving the ends free as arms, and securing it with glue. This leaves no extra to turn up for hands, which is fine if sleeves are to cover them.

If you have a vise, it is simple to drill a small hole through the shoulders and push the pipe cleaner through (Fig. 6-15). The arms are then flexible and there's no worry about the glue not holding.

Another alternative is a medium- to heavy-gauge florist wire or craft wire, which can be cut to any length, doubled at the hands, and wound twice around the body to secure it (Fig. 6-16). Wrap it with flesh-colored bias binding; this makes a very neat hand.

Paint hair and face on the top of the doll (be sure to include the traditional red dots on the cheeks, which have characterized clothespin dolls for generations). If her feet are to show, dip the bottom in black paint to look like shoes.

Cut blouse (see pattern, Fig. 6-17), from fabric folded at the shoulders. Sew lace to cuffs of sleeves. Stitch underarm seams from waist to cuff; gather neck. Turn, put on doll, and pull neck tight. Cut a 3x7-inch rectangle for skirt and hem along one long side, adding a row of lace or trim if desired. Stitch side seam, gather waist, and put on doll upside down and inside out, so it covers her head.

Stitch waist to shirt tail securely and bring skirt down to cover legs. An apron or a ribbon sash may be

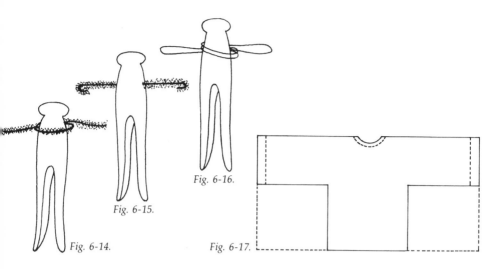

Fig. 6-16.

Fig. 6-15.

Fig. 6-14.

Fig. 6-17.

added at the waist. Gather a short length of lace and stitch to the neck of the dress to form a collar.

Pantalets are traditional on clothespin dolls, and they are simply two cylinders of fabric with lace trim at the bottom ends or two pieces of wide eyelet trim. Slip them onto the doll's legs and secure to inside of dress with a few stitches.

You can vary her costume greatly. Wide lace or very wide ribbon or trim makes beautiful dresses and aprons that don't need hemming. Aprons can also be cut on the bias to make hemming unnecessary. She can have yarn hair or a matching button (remove shank first) glued atop her head as a topknot. All manner of tiny scraps of ribbon and lace can adorn her.

If she is to be a display doll, you may want her to have an attractive pedestal, such as a sawed section of 1-inch-diameter tree branch (birch is especially pretty). For a doll house, her height is important, so it is best to glue her feet to a large flat button. This gives her a firm footing, so she doesn't have to depend on her skirt alone to hold her up.

For little girls who collect dolls, you might dress clothespin dolls in the costumes of famous people or characters such as Betsy Ross, Martha Washington, Little Red Riding Hood, Topsy, or Heidi.

Beanbag

Beanbags may be made from nearly any close-woven fabric (including knit), but those made from fleece or fur fabrics are especially appealing to younger children. While a simple square or circle will do, a beanbag in a special shape is more fun to play with (Fig. 6-19).

For a cat face, cut two pieces from fleece fabric (Fig. 6-18) and embroider the face on one. A simple outline stitch will do, but the face will show up best on a thick pile fabric if it is embroidered in satin stitch (see p. 41, Fig. 5-15, for diagrams of stitches). Sew the two pieces together, right sides facing, leaving the space between the ears open for turning. Stitch close to the edge and use a zigzag machine stitch or sew around it twice using a running stitch. This gives it extra strength to avoid leaks.

Turn and fill the bag loosely with millet seed, which is fine and smooth and will not choke a child who tries to sample it if the bag breaks. You can buy this at health-food stores or wherever birdseed is sold. (Don't use millet intended for planting, since it may have been treated with chemicals.) Sew the opening with a double set of overcast stitches.

A bucket or basket of brightly colored beanbags makes a good gift.

Tossing the beanbags into the bucket is fun for one or several children, and also helps improve coordination. Older children will make up their own games and rules to suit their skills, while little ones will be content to just be able to throw the bags into the bucket.

Puppet

Puppets are fun for nearly any age, especially if they are easy for

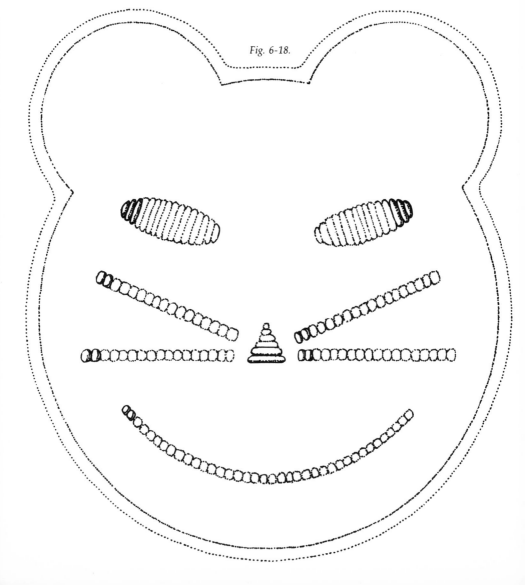

Fig. 6-18.

Fig. 6-19. *Scraps of fleece fabric are perfect for small beanbags (made by Dee Radcliffe).*

little hands to use. Since puppets with hard heads and finger holes for operating the hands are too cumbersome for very small children, a simple felt puppet with a big mouth is a better choice (Fig. 6-20).

To make an alligator puppet, cut front, back, face, and two arms from green felt (Figs. 6-21 through 6-24). Cut mouth (Fig. 6-25) and two eyes (Fig. 6-26) from red, and two hands (Fig. 6-27) from light blue or a different shade of green. Cut two strips of white felt ⅝ inch wide and 12 inches long. Snip each into a long row of teeth by cutting notches along one edge (Fig. 6-28).

Sew teeth all around edge of mouth, stitching as close to the edge as possible. Embroider black centers in eyes and appliqué eyes to face as shown. To make eyes bulge slightly, tuck half a cotton ball under each before stitching is completed. Embroider two red nostrils on snout (Fig. 6-23).

Fold arms lengthwise, insert hands at one end of each, and stitch open sides. All stitching is done on top, wrong sides together. Pin arms to top side of alligator back (Fig. 6-

22). Stitch top of mouth to face around snout (A. to A.). Stitch bottom of mouth to front piece (B. to B.). Stitch back to assembled face and front (C. to C.), leaving bottom edges open and stitching arms into body as you close the side seams. Trim edges if necessary so stitching is at the very edge.

Since all stitching shows, be sure your threads match the felt on which you are sewing. When stitching the mouth to the face and front, use white thread on tooth edge and green thread in the bobbin.

You can change the personality of the alligator by just moving the centers of his eyes, or changing their shape slightly. Such differences in detail also help each child in the same family identify his own puppet if you make several.

Block Puzzle

Those who are happier working with wood than with fabric can also make delightful toys.

Among the oldest is a block puzzle. You will need six colorful pictures on good, heavy paper, and they must be the same size. (You can, of course, use parts of larger ones trimmed to the size required.) A pictorial calendar is a good source. The pictures should be at least 6 inches square. They can be any size actually, but keep in mind that anything over 9x12 inches is hard to work with. You will need a piece (or pieces) of 2x6 or 2x8 board and a good saw. (If you are purchasing the wood, ask for it by these measurements, although they are not the actual finished dimensions.)

Sand both sides well. Measure the thickness of the wood *exactly*. Mark your picture off in squares exactly

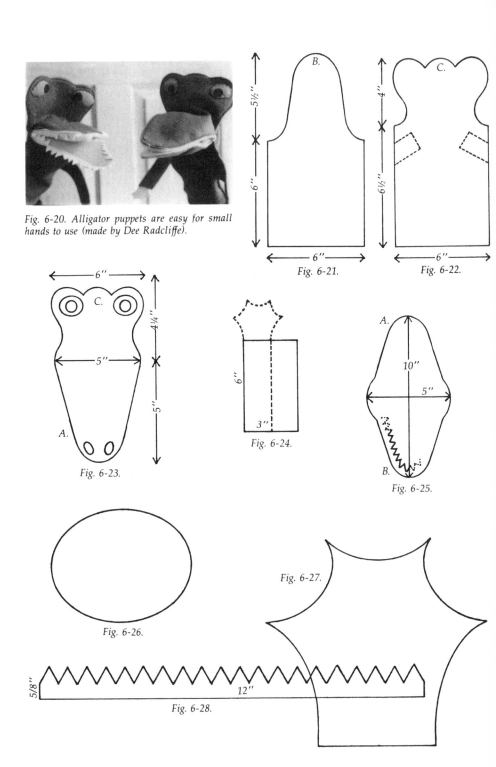

Fig. 6-20. Alligator puppets are easy for small hands to use (made by Dee Radcliffe).

B.

5½"

6"

6"

Fig. 6-21.

C.

4"

6½"

6"

Fig. 6-22.

6"

C.

4¼"

5"

5"

A.

Fig. 6-23.

6"

3"

Fig. 6-24.

A.

10"

5"

B.

Fig. 6-25.

Fig. 6-26.

Fig. 6-27.

5/8"

12"

Fig. 6-28.

the thickness of the wood. Count the squares in one picture, and mark your wood off into the same number of squares. Be sure to allow for the width of the saw cut. The blocks must be exactly the same size as the picture squares.

Cut the wood into cubes (they should be perfect cubes if you measured right), and sand smooth any and all rough or splintered corners or edges.

From here on, keeping your pictures separate is essential. Cut one picture at a time into squares on the measured lines and glue each square to the face of one cube, keeping the squares in order, until each square of the first picture has been glued to a wooden cube. Now turn each cube once in the same direction and glue the next picture on in order. Continue for the remaining four sides. Let glue dry overnight or longer.

Using clear varnish or polymer spray, coat the puzzle blocks one side at a time, allowing the finish to dry after each coating. If you are especially handy, you can make an open wooden box for the blocks to go into. Or find a cardboard box to exactly fit the puzzle. Place the blocks in the box so that one picture is complete.

Mitten Rack

Any child who lives where snow fills the winter would welcome his own mitten rack, on which mittens can be hung to dry before the next outing.

The rack can be nearly any shape or size and hold any number of mittens. (After a wet snow we have as many as three pairs of each size dry-

ing at once.) For a sturdy base use a piece of board about ¾ inch thick. Make a pattern for a design you like — a heart, snowman (draw around a tea cup and a saucer, overlapping slightly, for a pattern), fish, pig, or any other attractive design. If you are adept with a saw, you might even cut out a child's initial (or initials).

Cut the design from the wood, sand edges, and mark two evenly aligned points (or more on a larger rack) at least 3 inches apart. Using a ½-inch bit, drill holes not quite all the way through the wood.

Cut two 4-inch sections of ½-inch dowel. Sand one end of each dowel to round it off smoothly. Sand the edges of the drilled holes to remove any roughness and put a few drops of wood glue into the holes. Place the unfinished ends of the dowels in

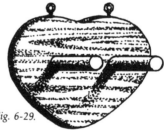

Fig. 6-29.

the holes, pushing firmly until they are in place. Let glue dry.

Stain lightly if desired and finish with a urethane or other waterproof finish. If the grain rises, sand lightly between coats, since the pegs must not have any rough spots. When the finish is dry, put two screw eyes in the top for hanging (Fig. 6-29).

Although simple in design, these gifts are sure to delight the children on your Christmas list.

GIFTS FOR CHILDREN TO MAKE

Read This First!

BEFORE you start to make any of these pretty and useful gifts, read *all* the directions for it. Be sure you have everything you need. Also, be sure it's all right to use all the tools, like the sewing machine, or ask someone else to work with you on these parts of the directions.

If you have trouble, keep trying, ask for help, and try to be patient. Remember that all the projects shown in the pictures were done by children. We've mentioned their ages just so you'll see what even very young people can do if they really try!

Look in other parts of the book for things you can make, too, like corn-husk dolls, tissue-paper wreaths, and many other decorations and gifts.

Pine-Cone Fire Starters

If you live in New England, or another area where white-pine trees grow, you can gather bags of cones for your friends who have fireplaces. Other large cones will do, but those with a lot of pitch on them are the best. (Pitch is the sticky substance on pine trees and other evergreens.)

You can tell a white pine by the number of needles it has in each little cluster: if there are five long needles (one for each letter in WHITE), it's a white pine. Its cones are long and just right to put in a fireplace, since the pitch on them will burn long enough to get the kindling started.

Gather the cones and let them dry out (they will open up and be quite crisp). Cut a piece of nylon net — we use red — into a 24-inch square. Put a dozen or so pine cones in the middle and pull the corners up. Tie the bundle with colored ribbon and make a tag that says "Fire Starters." Anyone with a fireplace will be glad to receive that for Christmas!

Berry Bowl

Another gift to make using nature's materials is a berry bowl. Look in the first chapter for pictures of partridgeberry and teaberry. If these grow in your woods, gather a small plastic bag full. Be sure to get a few clumps of nice green moss, too. Keep them in a plastic bag with a few drops of water until you use them.

You will need a glass rose bowl, which looks like a small round fish bowl. You can buy it from the florist or find it at a yard sale. Be sure the bowl is sparkling clean, then place a layer of moss, green side down, on the bottom. Put in the little berry vines, gently pressing the tiny roots loosely into the soil that came with the moss roots.

Spread the berry vines around the inside so they are near the wall of the bowl. Make sure the berries show. Put a teaberry plant in the center of the bowl so its leaves drape over the top of the partridgeberry. The bowl should be fairly full. Sprinkle a little water in it if the plants are dry.

If your bowl doesn't have a lid, cut a piece of clinging plastic wrap into a circle about 2 inches bigger than the top of the bowl and cover the opening with it, pressing it down so it will stick. If your bowl has a rim on it, you can tie a red ribbon around the top, too. Because the water can't escape, the plants will stay green for a long time.

Covered Coat Hanger

Have you ever tried to hang up a blouse or shirt and had it slip off the hanger onto the floor? I'm sure your mother has, and you can make her a gift to solve that problem! (See Fig. 7-1.) This project takes a little bit of time, but it is quite easy to do.

To cover a coat hanger you will need two wire hangers exactly alike, a skein of rug yarn or bulky knitting yarn rolled into a ball, and masking tape.

Put the two hangers together to make one hanger and tape them together in two or three places. Begin at the "stem" (the straight section below the part that curls over the closet rod) and tie the yarn tightly to it in a knot.

Then start making a series of "half hitches." To make a half hitch, lay the hanger on your lap or on the table and hold the yarn ball in your left hand. Unroll about 12 inches of yarn and hold it out from the hanger on the left side. Take the ball of yarn in your right hand, but keep the long piece of yarn in your left hand as you unroll more, and move the ball to the right side of the hanger stem.

Now you have a big loop in your left hand and the ball in your right hand. Pass the ball of yarn under the stem and pull it toward you *through* the loop of yarn. Pull it tight just below the first knot, and you'll see it make another neat little knot. Keep making these down the stem, pulling each one tight, until you reach the main part of the coat hanger.

Fig. 7-1. Coat hangers padded with yarn are perfect for special blouses and dresses (made by Kristine and Scott Stepenuck, ages 8 and 6).

Start making knots around the main part of the hanger, passing the ball through the center of the hanger instead of behind the stem. When you have gone all the way around, end the yarn by tying a double knot, and cut it off.

To decorate your hanger, tie a bow around the stem, using about 12 inches of satin ribbon that matches the yarn.

Sachets

You might want to tie a spicy-smelling sachet to your coat hanger to keep your mother's closet smelling nice. Or you can give sachets as a separate gift.

The fabric you choose can be cotton gingham or calico, striped, printed, or plain; but it should be thin enough to fold easily and the print or stripe should be small.

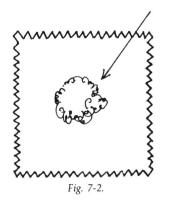

Fig. 7-2.

Fig. 7-3.

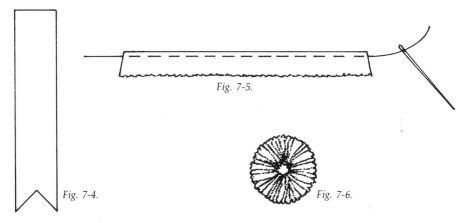

Fig. 7-5.

Fig. 7-4.

Fig. 7-6.

Heavy fabrics like wool or knits don't work well.

Cut a 6-inch square for each sachet, using pinking shears if you have them. Lay the square wrong side up on a table and put about a teaspoonful of whole cloves in the center (Fig. 7-2). Pull the corners up to make a bundle and tie it tightly with a 6-inch strip of narrow lace or ribbon. Pull the corners out so they look perky and pretty (Fig. 7-3).

If you plan ahead a little, you can make sachets of dried orange peel mixed with cloves. Just save the peel from an orange and tear it into little pieces. Spread them in a pie tin and leave them in a warm, dry place until they are snappy and crisp. (A radiator, top of the refrigerator, and the shelf of a wood cook stove are all good places.) Use half peel and half cloves for sachet filling.

Bookmarks

No matter how old or how young you are, you can make pretty book-marks. You will need an 8- to 10-inch piece of ribbon (any width) for each. Cut the bottom into an inverted "V" shape (Fig 7-4).

There are many things you can use to decorate the top of the book-mark: a small picture, for example, cut neatly out of a greeting card or other firm paper (magazine paper is too thin). Carefully glue the picture to the top of the ribbon with white glue. Use only a drop, and then hold the picture and ribbon together with your thumb and forefinger until the glue is set.

Or you can cut small shapes (see patterns, Fig. 7-7) from felt and either glue or sew them to the rib-bon. If you have a small scrap of lace, gather it by running a threaded needle through it in big stitches. Leave enough thread on both ends of the lace (Fig. 7-5) so you can pull the ends to form a circle (Fig. 7-6). Tie the thread ends tightly and sew the lace circle to the ribbon. Cover the center with a bright button or pompom or a dot of felt. You might want to add a green felt leaf to your lace "flower."

A nice bookmark for a friend or relative you don't see often is one with a small photograph of yourself. You can "frame" it by gluing strips of narrow ribbon around it. Then glue the ribbon-framed photo to the bookmark ribbon. Be *very* sparing with the glue so you don't drown the photo or the bookmark in it!

Fig. 7-7.

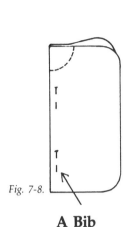

Fig. 7-8.

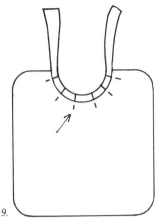

Fig. 7-9.

A Bib

Do you have a baby brother or sister or cousin you'd like to make a present for? You can make a very pretty bib out of a washcloth. Choose one that's a bright color. You'll also need a 20-inch piece of "double fold" bias tape in a color that matches or looks pretty with the washcloth.

Fold the washcloth carefully in half and pin it to hold it in place. Have someone help you with the next step because the cloth is hard to cut! Cut a "bite" shaped piece out of the folded corner (Fig. 7-8). It should be about 2½ inches wide and 2½ inches deep. Unpin the edges and open the washcloth.

Pin the double fold bias tape over the cut edge, leaving two long "tails" the same length (Fig. 7-9). If you can use a sewing machine, stitch the tape in place (a zigzag sewing machine stitch is easiest). You can also stitch it very neatly by hand, being careful to make each stitch go through both the washcloth and the front and back of the tape. Be sure to knot the thread ends tightly before you cut them off.

If you are very good with a sewing machine, you might like to stitch a ruffle of gathered eyelet lace around the outer edge of the bib. This would make a beautiful bib for a baby sister!

A String Can

Almost everyone needs a place to keep wrapping string. Your dad's workshop, the kitchen — every house has a ball of string or twine somewhere, and usually it's coming unwound.

With a clean 1-pound coffee can and its lid, plus a piece of pretty paper or cloth and some white glue, you can make a string can. Old wallpaper scraps or samples, pretty gift wrap, or a leftover piece of heavy curtain material works fine.

Cut a piece of fabric or paper 5¼x13½ inches. Be sure to cut the edges straight — a ruler will help. Glue the paper or fabric to the can, pressing the edges tightly and smoothing out all wrinkles. Leave the top and bottom rims of the can showing. Or if you want to be fancy, you can glue a strip of narrow ribbon or rickrack around the top and bottom of the can. Be sure to put the lid on the can first before gluing on the ribbon or rickrack, so the trim doesn't get in the way when the lid snaps on.

With the plastic lid on the can, have someone help you punch a hole right in the middle of the lid. Use the points of a pair of scissors. Remove the lid and trim the hole as smoothly as possible. It needs only to be large enough for the end of the string or twine to pass through.

Storage Cans

Other cans can be covered without the lids to make attractive holders for wooden spoons, scissors, pencils, toothbrushes, screwdrivers, and small tools or nails. Cover the can just as you did for the string holder, but cover the top rim with ribbon or trim (Fig. 7-10).

Pincushions

With a wide ribbon or pretty embroidered trim, you can make beautiful pincushions. Cut a piece of ribbon or trim twice as long as it is wide, plus 1 inch. (For example: if the trim is 3 inches wide, cut a length 3+3+1, or 7 inches long.)

Fold it in half with right sides together, and sew the *cut* edges together, making a ½-inch seam. Sew one of the bound edges, too, by stitching right along the edge. Turn it right side out, stuff it tightly with polyfiber filling, and stitch the last edge closed, using tiny stitches that go over and over the edge. Be sure your thread matches the ribbon or trim!

To be extra fancy, make a little bow of narrow ribbon and sew it to one corner. Stick in a few pins, and your pincushion is ready to wrap up and give!

Another type of pincushion can be made by sewing two 4-inch squares or circles of pretty cloth together (with right sides facing), leaving a 2-inch space open. Turn

Fig. 7-10. Cans of any size become attractive containers when covered with wallpaper (made by Amy and Jim Gibbons, ages 9 and 7).

right side out, stuff, and sew closed with neat little stitches. Find a pretty button and sew it with a double thread to the very center, right through the whole pincushion, pulling the thread very tight, so it makes a dent in the middle of the pincushion. Tie a good strong knot on the bottom before you cut the thread tails.

Dustmop

This is a long project, but an easy one to hide away in a paper bag and work on whenever you have a minute. You will need a wire coat hanger, two skeins of rug yarn in colors that look nice together, a piece of cardboard 4½x10 inches, and a pair of scissors. (Rug yarn works best because it picks up the dust instead of just pushing it around.)

Have someone help you wind the rug yarn into two balls. Then neatly

Fig. 7-11. Dustmops can be made in colors to match a kitchen — this one is red, blue, green, and white to match curtain fabric (made by Julie Rogers, age 9).

Fig. 7-12.

Fig. 7-13.

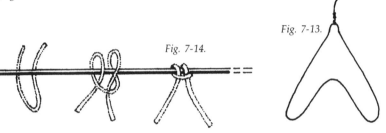

Fig. 7-14.

wrap the yarn around the short side of the cardboard until the cardboard is covered with one layer. Slide one blade of the scissors under the yarn and cut along one long edge of the cardboard (Fig. 7-12). You will have a lot of 9-inch pieces of yarn. Do the same thing with the other ball of yarn.

Bend the coat hanger down on the ends and up in the middle, as shown in Fig. 7-13. Begin at the stem of the coat hanger, just below the round part that curls around the closet rod. Fold a 9-inch piece of yarn in half, lay it against the coat hanger, and pull the ends through the folded loop end (Fig. 7-14). Pull tight. You will have a little knot with two tails. Repeat, using the other color yarn. Push it close to the first one and keep making more, changing colors each time. Go down the stem and all

around both loops of the coat hanger. Keep pushing the loops close together. When you are all the way around, take a long piece of yarn and tie it to the handle just where you started the loops. Very neatly, wrap it around the curved part, right to the end, so the hanger is all covered. Glue the yarn at the end and cut it off. The curved end is the handle and is also a handy way to hang up the dustmop (Fig. 7-11).

Even mothers who hate to dust (like me!) will enjoy using this because it reaches into hard places, like between the rungs on chair backs and into corners.

When you make pretty, useful gifts like these, you not only have the fun of making and giving them, but you will see them used and enjoyed, too!

CARDS, TAGS, AND GIFT WRAPS

Fig. 8-1. Plain and fancy gift papers and colorful fabrics make bags to conceal hard-to-wrap gifts.

PRESENTING gifts in attractive wrappings has been a tradition for many generations. Wrappings not only serve to hide the gift until it is time to open it, but become decorations in their own right. A basket of wrapped gifts lends a colorful accent to any room, and the jumble of bright presents piled under the tree is part of any child's anticipation of Christmas.

Gift Wrap

Both children and adults can make unusual and beautiful wrap- ping paper. Plain white tissue paper and heavier white or cream-colored paper stock are the best to use as a base for decorating.

The only other materials needed are a few medium-sized, washed potatoes; biscuit cutter (or small round cookie cutter); paring knife; pencil with an unused eraser; red and green tempera paints or ink pads; and paint brushes.

Cut a potato in half lengthwise so you have two ovals. Place them cut sides down on a chopping board and go around the edge with the

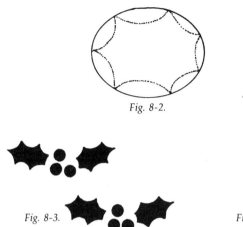

Fig. 8-2.

Fig. 8-3.

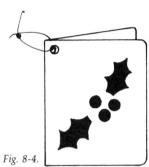

Fig. 8-4.

biscuit cutter, taking out bite-shaped sections (Fig. 8-2) to make a holly leaf.

Thin some green tempera paint and brush it onto cut surfaces of the potato. To print, press the painted or inked surface firmly on the paper to be decorated. Try printing on a sheet of newspaper first, until you get used to how many prints you can get from one brushing of paint. It varies according to the moisture in the potato, consistency of the paint, and absorbency of the paper. Adjust the paint (how much you brush on, how thin it is, etc.) until you can print holly leaves that you like.

If you have ink pads, use the potatoes like a rubber stamp. This is much faster, but does not give quite as bright a print.

Spread several layers of newspaper on a table and put a double layer of tissue paper over them (or use a single layer of heavier paper). Print your holly leaves in pairs at random, in staggered rows, or however you like them. To add berries, use the pencil eraser, brushed with red

tempera or ink, as the stamp (Fig. 8-3). Spread paper out to dry, or hang it over a towel rack.

You can make matching gift tags by cutting plain white typing paper into rectangles twice the size of your potato, allowing a little extra room for a margin. Fold in half and print a single leaf and a few berries on the front of each. Punch a hole in the corner and tie red string or narrow ribbon through the hole (Fig. 8-4).

Christmas Cards

Christmas cards are made in the same way, using white drawing paper or other sturdy, hard-surfaced paper. Since envelopes can be a problem, make your cards to fit the sizes available — measure the envelope and subtract ½ inch each way to determine folded-card size. Cut the paper twice the shortest dimension so you can fold it.

You can make more elaborate designs, even short words, by carving your design into the potato with a sharp knife, leaving the cut surface flat wherever you want the color to print. Remember to make mirror-image letters (reversed), so they will be right when printed (Fig. 8-5). "Joy" is a good word for a potato print, as is "Noel." More than four letters gets a little cramped on one potato! Or you can carve single letters out of potato halves and print each separately. For the inside of a card, each letter in "Joy" could be carved on a potato half (a separate potato half for each letter) and printed one letter at a time. On wrapping paper, each letter can be printed at a jaunty angle in alternating colors.

Other designs you might try are a candy cane (print only the red stripes), a tree, a bell, or a star. These are quite simple to carve with a paring knife.

If you plan to print one design in several colors, cut a separate potato half for each color.

When wrapping with the printed tissue, use a sheet of plain white tissue underneath to make the paper more opaque and make your design show up better.

Fabric Cards and Package Decorations

Fabric cutouts glued to paper make very pretty Christmas cards and package decorations. For these, starch some scraps of gingham, calico, stripes, and solids in cotton and blended fabrics. Use only thin, woven fabrics — no knits. Iron them smooth and cut out letters or simple designs (trace around cookie cutters for patterns).

Let the fabric suggest the design: green Christmas trees and holly leaves, brown gingerbread boys, gold bells and stars, red bows, etc. Most such designs are symmetrical, so that you can cut them by folding the fabric in half and cutting half the pattern on the folded fabric.

Thin some white glue with an equal amount of water and brush it *very* thinly and quickly on the wrong side of the fabric cutout. It needn't cover every little space. Place right side up on the front of the folded card (use artists' paper or a folded plain white 3x5 index card). Press down all over with a soft

Fig. 8-5.

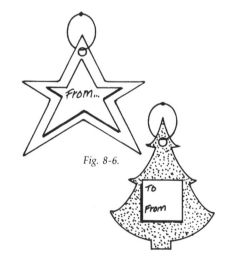

Fig. 8-6.

absorbent cloth and quickly wipe off any glue that might have seeped out onto the paper. Keep a damp cloth handy to wipe off excess glue.

For fabric package decorations, wrap the gift in white or in solid-colored, glossy-finish wrapping paper (Hallmark makes a good one). Glue fabric design to package in the same way.

Starched fabric cutouts can be used for tags, too, by cutting a small piece of white paper and gluing it to the center of the fabric. The white paper can be square or the same shape as the fabric cutout (Fig. 8-6). On a large flat package, try repeating a larger design in miniature for the tag.

Wrapping Bags

Wrapping bags of colorful fabric or paper can solve various gift-wrapping problems (Fig. 8-1).

Fabric Bags: Fabric bags are especially handy for wrapping long, thin bottles; long-handled kitchen utensils; and other odd shapes that defy the principles of box wrapping.

Cut two rectangles of bright-colored fabric (red-and-white stripe is nice) and place right sides together. Stitch together on all but one short side to form a bag (Fig. 8-7). Be sure the combined width is at least 2 inches greater than the measurement around the object to be enclosed, and its length greater by about 6 inches.

Either hem the top or trim with pinking shears. Turn right side out, put the gift in the bag, and tie closed with matching narrow rickrack, gold cord, or ribbon (Fig. 8-8). Besides being a solution for gift-wrapping, the bag is reusable — you might even get it back next year!

Paper Bags: Paper gift bags are also useful, reusable, and not difficult to make. The best material is a sturdy gift-wrap paper in a design appropriate to the size of the bag.

You can make these bags in any size or proportion from 1 inch wide to shopping-bag size, but for your first one, try a 2x6½-inch bag. You will need an 8x9-inch rectangle of gift wrap and a 2-inch square of cardboard. For this size bag, thin cardboard will do nicely. White glue, a ruler, and a pencil are the only other necessities. It may also help to have a flat-bottomed brown paper bag — a lunch bag or grocery-store bag — as an example, so you can see how the ends are folded in.

Measure your paper on the reverse side and draw faint lines beginning ½ inch from each 8-inch end and then spacing 2 inches apart as shown in Fig. 8-9. Number and letter the sections lightly about 2 inches from the top.

Measure 1¼ inches up from the bottom and mark a line lightly. Measure ½ inch down from the top

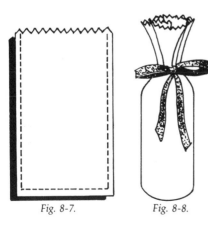

Fig. 8-7.   Fig. 8-8.

and mark again. Fold this top ½ inch toward you (so the printed side shows on the reverse side) and glue it firmly. This will be the top edge of the bag.

Fold in the same direction along all the vertical lines so the printed side of the paper is out. You will have a long chimney-shaped piece with ½-inch seams folded in. Crease all the folds and unfold the paper. Fold up on the bottom line, crease, and unfold.

Fold sides 2 and 4 in half vertically toward the *reverse* side of the paper (Fig. 8-10). This is opposite the direction of all other folds. Crease. This pleat will be the gusset that allows the bag to fold. Unfold the paper again.

On sides 2 and 4, measure a point on the center crease 1 inch above the bottom fold and mark with a pencil dot. Draw a light line from there to each of the bottom fold corners (Fig. 8-11). The line should dent the paper just enough to provide a fold line. Push upward from the printed side (which is down) toward you at the dot in the gusset crease and encourage the paper to fold on the diagonal line. Pinch this crease with your fingers.

On side 1, draw a line horizontally 1 inch above the bottom fold (the same height as the dots). Push this line upward and pinch to form a crease (Fig. 8-11). This is where the bag will fold.

Below the bottom fold on sides 1 and 3, measure the center at the bottom edge and make a mark. Draw lines from the top corners of the bottom fold to this mark on the edge (Fig. 8-12) and crease outward along these lines. These will be the flaps that give your bag a neat bottom. These creases will be firmed later, but by determining their position now, you insure a neat miter.

Refold the bag along the vertical lines and glue the two seam flaps A and B face to face, inside the bag. Then glue this seam toward the

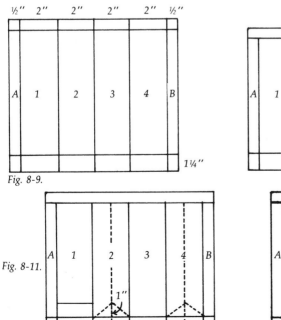

Fig. 8-9.

Fig. 8-11.

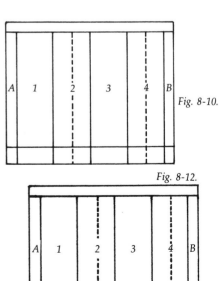

Fig. 8-10.

Fig. 8-12.

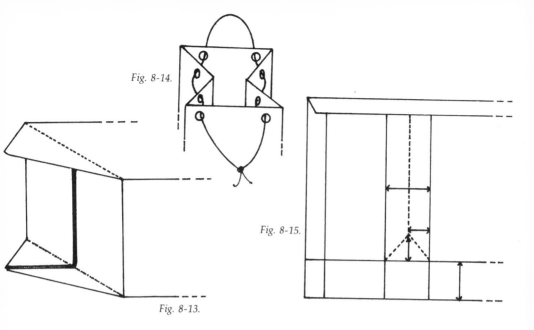

Fig. 8-14.

Fig. 8-15.

Fig. 8-13.

gusseted panel (4) so it is flat against the inside. It will now be folded as a part of panel 4.

Fold the bottom points along previously creased lines, and fold in the bottom edges neatly (Fig. 8-13). Stand the bag up and glue a cardboard square inside the bottom of the bag. Hold the cardboard down firmly with the eraser end of a long pencil inserted into the bag until the glue sets. (If you're making a larger bag, you can put your hand inside to hold it.) Glue the triangular flaps down over outside bag bottom and hold firmly as before until glue sets (Fig. 8-13).

Push inward at triangular creases on sides of bag, folding bag flat along these lines and the crease across side 1. Do this slowly and stop if the fold is not following the creases you made earlier. You can ease the folds into the right places quite easily. When the bag is flat, press it with your hands so it will remain creased in the right places. After that, it can be folded and

unfolded as needed and still retain its shape. Erase the numbers inside.

Punch a hole through all four layers in two places at the top edge of the bag (Fig. 8-14). Holes should line up when the bag folds. Put a cord through one set and back through the other set; tie it to form a continuous loop.

Once you have completed one bag and understand the way the bottom is assembled, you can vary the size and shape of the bag infinitely. When the bottom of the bag is not square, sides 2 and 4 (the gusseted panels) should be the narrower ones. The distance between the bottom fold line and the gusset fold point is half the width of the narrow (gusseted) side (Fig. 8-15). The bottom fold is this same measurement plus ¼ inch.

Your beautiful handmade gifts deserve special wrappings — and what could be more appropriate than paper, containers, and tags you've made yourself?

THE TREE TRIMS

Fig. 9-1. A wreath of salt clay can be made small enough for a tree ornament or large enough to hang on the wall.

OUR tree is a treasury of folk art — a showcase for hand-made decorations, especially those made by family and friends. The collection is added to constantly. Almost every craft can be used in one way or another to fashion a traditional Christmas tree ornament — origami, cornhusk and applehead dolls, dried flowers, paper quilling, quilting, and salt-clay modeling.

Patchwork Ball

Tree trims can often be made with the scraps left from larger projects! Take the pieces of calico or more elegant fabrics left over from quilting or sewing, and use them for cheerful patchwork balls (Fig. 9-2).

Even the tiniest scraps can be glued in a crazy-quilt pattern over Styrofoam balls to make cheerful patchwork ornaments. Use white glue and apply it thinly to the ball, working in one small area at a time. Cover any messy edges with bits of rickrack or ribbon. For smoother edges, give thinner fabrics a quick dose of spray starch before you cut them.

Patchwork balls can also be made without glue. Begin by pushing the edges of a fabric scrap straight into the Styrofoam with the rounded tip of a dinner knife. Do the adjoining edge of the next piece first and then tuck in the rest of it. Continue until the ball is covered.

Push very narrow lace into any

depressions where the edge has either frayed or been pulled out, and in any other places needed to balance the lace effect. You don't want lace just on one side. Finish the ball with a hanger of "invisible" thread secured to the top with a straight pin, and a long-tailed bow of narrow ribbon or lace attached also with a pin.

Wreath Ornaments

Fabric Wreath Ornaments: Scraps can also be used to make a wreath-shaped ornament (Fig. 9-2). Cut out about a dozen circles of calico or gingham fabric. (Trace around the top of a drinking glass.) Gather each circle around the outer edge, turning under a very narrow hem as you gather. Put two or three cotton balls in the middle of each circle and pull, gathering tightly, to form a firm little puff (Fig. 9-3). Tie gathering securely.

Thread these puffs in facing pairs (gathers together) on a very stout thread, pushing the needle right through the center of each, as though you were stringing beads (Fig. 9-4). Push them together very tightly and knot the thread.

Bring them around to form a circle and bring the thread through the first two or three puffs again to tighten the circle. Knot the thread and cut it. You may have to take a few small stitches with regular sewing thread to pull the balls together and tuck in edges that show. Sew on a tiny bow, and finish with a loop of invisible thread for the hanger.

Salt Clay Wreath Ornaments: Another type of wreath ornament to hang on the tree or on a cupboard

Fig. 9-2. Tiny scraps of calicos make this patchwork tree ornament and tiny wreath. (Wreath by Bonnie Gibbons.)

Fig. 9-3.

Fig. 9-4.

door for a festive touch is one made from salt clay (Fig. 9-1). Salt clay is inexpensive, easy to use, and well suited to small ornaments. Use it to make a wreath ornament anywhere from 3 to 8 inches in diameter. For large wreaths, work directly on a cookie sheet, since you may have trouble moving them. A recipe for salt clay follows.

SALT CLAY

4 cups flour
1 cup salt
1½ cups lukewarm water

Mix flour and salt and add water. Mix well and knead about 10 minutes. It will be sticky at first, but will become more like clay as you knead it. Keep wrapped in plastic, taking out only as much as you need at one time.

Form a coil of dough long enough to go around the size circle you want. Lay it in a perfect circle by putting a glass or small bowl in the center and placing the clay around it. Remove the glass and press the dough fairly flat with your thumbs; if there are deep, heavy areas, the dough will bake unevenly and crack.

Roll or press a quantity of clay flat to about the thickness of pie crust. With a small knife, cut out a large number of leaf-shaped pieces varying slightly in size and shape. For a wreath 3 inches in diameter, the leaves should be no longer than ¼ inch — bigger proportionately for a larger ring.

Press these onto the ring of dough so that the tips of one row cover the base of the previous one. Don't line them up in neat rows; instead, place them casually, but keep the wreath well-balanced.

Fig. 9-5. Santa is a perfect subject for tree ornaments modeled from salt clay (made by Brenda Sherwin).

When the whole wreath is covered with leaves, form small pieces of fruit in appropriate sizes — apples, oranges, pears, bunches of grapes, a pineapple — and place them around the wreath. Moisten them just slightly on the back and press them gently into the leaves.

If you want a bow on your wreath, roll or cut a long flat strip of clay and fold it over to form a bow with two ends trailing slightly. "Tie" the bow at the center with a narrower strip of clay, and press the finished bow lightly into the dough at top or bottom of the wreath. Press a loop of wire (a cut hairpin will do) into the top of the wreath for a hanger.

Bake the wreath in a 300°F. oven for an hour or longer, until it is completely hard. Cool, and paint with acrylic artists' colors, using a very small brush for the fruit and

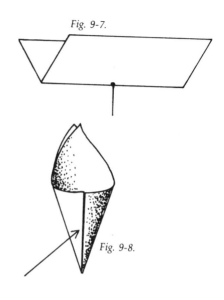

Fig. 9-7.

Fig. 9-8.

Fig. 9-6. Cornucopias may be made from paper or a quilted fabric.

bow. When paint is dry, spray with five or six coats (front and back) of clear polymer finish to seal.

Cornucopia

Paper or other cornucopias filled with candy or dried flowers have been favorite decorations since Victorian times. They are lovely and not at all difficult to make. The easiest version is made with an 8-inch square of writing paper, or strong gift wrap or parchment. Fold it in half to form a rectangle. Mark the center of the folded edge (Fig. 9-7); that will be the point, at the bottom. Roll the paper into a cone, wrapping it twice so the long pointed corners are together. Seal the outer edge with white glue (Fig. 9-8) and secure with a paper clip until dry. Decorate the edge by gluing on fabric trim, decorative tape, or ribbon. To hang, punch a hole in

the upstanding point at the top. A round-topped cornucopia is made in the same way from paper cut in a circle. If the paper is quite firm, you need use only a rectangle or half circle of paper instead of a square or full circle.

With firm materials, such as double-faced, quilted fabrics (Fig. 9-6), you need only cut a quarter circle (like a wide wedge of pie) and cover the rounded edge by stitching on bias tape or folded ribbon. Sew the straight sides together very close to the edge, and cover the raw edges with narrow ribbon, gold braid, or bias tape, hand stitched in place. Leave enough to form a loop at the top for hanging.

Sachets

Sachets make pretty, scented tree trims. Cut a 5-inch square of red gingham or calico, using pinking shears. Put a tablespoon of whole cloves in the center of the square. Draw the edges of the fabric up around the cloves and tie into a bundle with red or green ribbon (Fig. 9-9). Make a bow with short tails and use a loop of invisible thread for a hanger. Use this same type of sachet in place of a bow to decorate packages.

Hang miniature baskets full of cloves or Christmas potpourri on the tree. To make a sachet fit a round or square basket, cut a circle of fabric three times the diameter or the length of one side of the basket; for an oval or rectangular basket, cut the material three times the size of each dimension. Gather the outer edge and fill the fabric with spices or potpourri. Draw gathering thread tight and tie. Turn the bundle upside down and push it into the basket. Tie a bow of matching ribbon to the handle.

Pomander

Pomanders made of crab apples closely studded with whole cloves and allowed to dry a week or two or until hard make perfect little balls light enough to hang on a tree. Pin a bow of gingham ribbon and a loop of invisible thread into the stem end.

Fabric "Foods"

The first decorated Christmas tree on record appeared in Germany at about the time the first colonies began in America and was decorated with apples, candy treats, and paper flowers. Centuries later, Victorian trees were decked with candies and foods of every description, which in families with children were prone to disappear when no one was looking!

You can carry on the tradition of these early trees with more permanent decorations made from scraps and snippets of fabric, felt, and trim. But *this* pantry of goodies may be stored from year to year and won't hurt anyone's waistline!

Lollipop: Perhaps the easiest ornaments of this kind are calico-wrapped "lollipops." Begin with a round stick 4 inches long (save your fireplace matches), a 5-inch pinked square of fabric, a piece of ribbon,

Fig. 9-9. *Tiny colorful sachets add a spicy fragrance to the Christmas tree.*

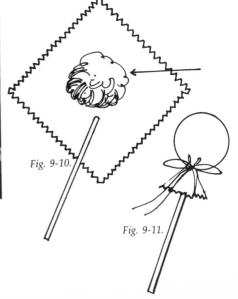

Fig. 9-10.

Fig. 9-11.

and several cotton balls. Place cotton balls in center of fabric (Fig. 9-10) and draw fabric edges around them. Put the stick in the center and secure with a small ribbon (Fig. 9-11).

Ribbon Candy: "Ribbon candy" is just that — ribbon! Thread a strip of stiff cotton ribbon back and forth onto a needle and invisible thread. Pull up to look like ribbon candy, tie a knot, and make a loop for hanging (Fig. 9-12). If ribbon is not reversible, use two pieces glued together so both sides are the same.

Gingerbread Man: You can also make permanent gingerbread men. Cut out in pairs from brown felt and glue each pair together with a loop of invisible thread in between. When the glue is dry, dab little dots of acrylic paint "frosting" on for the face and buttons (Fig. 9-13).

Ice Cream Cone: For an ice cream cone, glue a 4-inch square of yellow gingham to a piece of typing paper and cut into a quarter circle as for a cornucopia (Fig. 9-14). Fold into a cone shape, glue, and hold with a

Fig. 9-13. *Permanent gingerbread boys can be made of two layers of brown felt.*

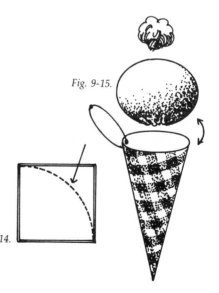

Fig. 9-15.

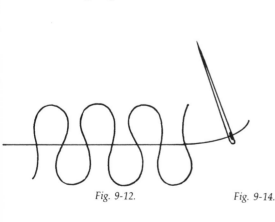

Fig. 9-12.

Fig. 9-14.

paper clip until it dries. Cut a 4-inch circle of solid-color pastel fabric. Gather around edge, stuff with cotton or polyfiber filling, and pull gathering to form a ball large enough to fit on the cone. Gathering need not be pulled to close the hole, as long as raw edges are inside cone. Knot and cut thread. Glue loop of invisible thread to seamed edge of cone and glue "ice cream" into cone with white glue. Glue a red pom-pom "cherry" on top of the ice cream (Fig. 9-15).

Candy Cane: A knitting spool is a gadget that looks like a jump rope handle with a large hole through its center and four small nails in the top. It is very inexpensive and can be purchased in any crafts supply or knitting shop. Directions come with it.

By knitting a 5-inch rope in alternating red and white stripes of knitting worsted (each stripe should be about 4 rows), you can make a candy cane. Simply bend a small loop in each end of a 5-inch piece of heavy florist wire and push it through the center of the rope. (The loops are there to prevent the cut ends from sticking out later.) Then bend rope into candy cane shape. Add a loop for hanging or simply hang the cane over a branch.

Fruits: Fabric fruits can be made from calicos, ginghams, or even velvets, but my favorites are from shiny fabrics like silks and satins. If you don't have scraps, you can buy short lengths of 3-inch satin ribbon and use it for fabric: ½ yard will make an apple, pear, and orange (and ⅔ yard of 2-inch ribbon will make leaves for all three); ¼ yard will make three strawberries.

Cut pattern pieces from satin rib-

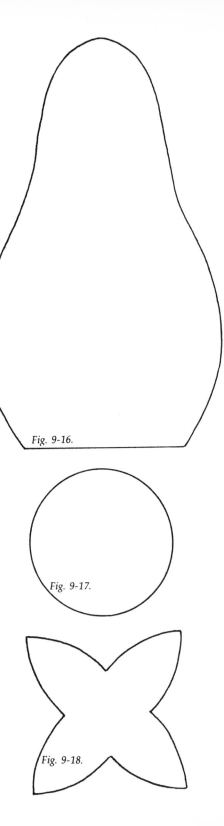

Fig. 9-16.

Fig. 9-17.

Fig. 9-18.

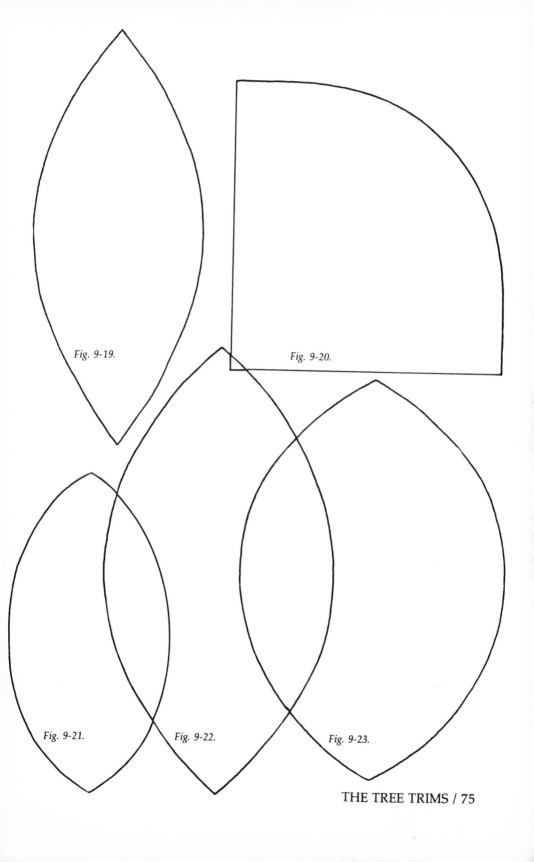

Fig. 9-19.

Fig. 9-20.

Fig. 9-21.

Fig. 9-22.

Fig. 9-23.

bon in quantity and colors indicated (Figs. 9-16 through 9-23).

Strawberry (Fig. 9-20): On the right side of the fabric make tiny stitches at random in yellow embroidery thread, for seeds. Fold with right sides together and stitch along straight side. Turn, stuff with polyfiber, and gather the top to close. Cut hull from felt (Fig. 9-18) and stitch into place.

Pear (Fig. 9-16): Stitch four sides together, right sides facing. Turn, stuff, and gather bottom edge loosely. Press under edges of circle (Fig. 9-17) and blind stitch to bottom. Stitch together leaf (Fig. 9-21), turn, and stitch to close, then sew to top of the pear.

Orange (Fig. 9-23): Stitch four pieces together, leaving half of the last seam open. Turn, stuff, and blind stitch to close. Make leaf (Fig. 9-19) as above and stitch to the orange.

Apple (Fig. 9-22): Stitch, stuff, and close as for orange. Using a stout thread and a long needle, draw a long stitch through the center of the apple (from bottom to top) and pull tight. Knot securely to hold the top of apple down in the center. Make leaf (Fig. 9-21) and attach it to stem end.

Make loops of invisible thread for all and attach to stem ends.

These fabric ornaments are permanent and don't have to be replaced each year, but a few tips on storage might be helpful. While they aren't breakable, some, like cornucopias and ribbon candy, will crush. These should be stored inside small boxes with other light ornaments, where they won't be crushed by larger or heavier pieces.

Wrapping each fabric ornament in tissue, as you would your glass ones, is also a good idea. If you leave your tree standing for several weeks, dust may gather on the fabric surfaces. Though it won't show for a year or two, after awhile it can dull their appearances. So before putting them away, dust them. A soft brush works well on the fruit and felt pieces. Cotton fabrics may even be brushed lightly with a slightly damp cloth.

Seed Pod Ornament

Milkweed pods can be used as frames for a number of small items, and their graceful shape hangs perfectly. Our favorite is a miniature arrangement of dried flowers set in a pod. Use a tiny piece of florist clay (that gummy strip they use to hold Styroblocks to the bottoms of vases) and press it inside the stem end of the pod. Into this base, stick short-stemmed straw flowers, small seed heads, and other dried materials to make an attractive arrangement. Cover the florist clay with a piece of dried moss or a single pine-cone scale. Glue a loop of invisible thread to the tip of the pod.

Other crafts described in this book can be made into Christmas tree ornaments; the crèche figures, festoons, pinchboxes, and calico bows all make interesting tree decorations. Countless other skills are easy to adapt; the potter, woodworker, tinsmith, even the baker can display miniature examples of his or her specialty on the Christmas tree.

THE TREE TRIM PARTY

THE traditions that surround trimming the Christmas tree are perhaps the most precious to each family. Some bring in and decorate the tree on Christmas Eve, after the children are asleep. What a surprise it must be to awaken and find a tree, as if by magic, all glowing and glittering!

Our family does it all together on an unhurried evening, after an early dinner. We spend hours unpacking decorations and placing them on the tree. It takes us a long time because we see these treasures only once a year, and each has special memories with its own stories to be told.

This is the occasion for giving "tree-trim presents," tree trims handmade or bought during the year with a particular member of the family in mind. The tree-trim presents are the first ornaments to go on the tree after the silver star. Although some (tall) people manage to "crown" their tree with the star as the grand finale, practicality suggests that on a large tree with fragile ornaments, crowning is best done first.

While every family seems to have its own ritual for trimming the tree, there is a vague order-of-business that makes it easier.

The tree should be set up to stand at least a couple of hours in the house before trimming begins. This gives it a chance to warm up, stretch, and have its limbs fall to their natural levels. Then you have a better idea of where to put what.

Because it is difficult to place lights on a tree hung with the ornaments, the lights should go on next. The heavy cord helps weigh down or hold up branches to fill in bare spots. If you use the tiny lights, they will balance easily, since there are so many. But larger lights may need quite a lot of moving about to keep them from being all in one place. Look at the tree from every angle to be sure they are well positioned.

If you are hanging garlands or chains, they should come next. Professional decorators who do those perfect trees in store windows have a few tricks with garlands that do help bring the tree together and frame the other ornaments. Your garlands may be tinsel, chains, or strings of beads, candy, popcorn, or cranberries. Begin draping garlands on the bottom branches and loop a heavy garland once around each branch that supports it. Leave plenty of drape — you don't want the garland to tie the tree up like a bundle. Put your largest and showiest ornaments in the places where the garlands intersect and let smaller ornaments be framed by the spaces. Plain glass balls should hang in toward the trunk, to give depth and reflect the light.

Hang the smallest ornaments from the very tips of branches, where they can be seen, or, for very small pieces, have a special table tree in the dining room. We have wooden angels less than an inch tall, tiny dolls, carved St. Nicholases, and a number of other ornaments that would be lost on the big tree; this table tree is the perfect place for them.

At our house, a third, "edible" tree is upstairs in the girls' room. It stands on their bureau, has tiny, red lights, and is decorated entirely with popcorn, frosted cookies, gingerbread boys, and candy canes. Occasionally other edible trim is added, but more often, these ornaments are subtracted — they disappear mysteriously.

While trimming the trees is strictly a family occasion with us, many different traditions accompany this festive opening of the holiday celebration. Tree-trim parties often include friends and neighbors, and all take turns adding ornaments.

One lovely idea friends had for a newly married couple was to give them a tree-trim party. All their friends arrived, each bearing an ornament for their first tree or a contribution of food to be eaten while trimming.

Carol singing adds to the fun — a cappella or along with a piano, organ, or even phonograph. Local newspapers often publish carols, both words and music, in a special Christmas section.

It's a time for festive foods whether the group is large or small. Hot mulled cider or wine is a nice accompaniment, along with some of the beautiful Christmas breads and sweets.

If the occasion is a family one, a fine way to end it is by reading a chapter of Charles Dickens' *A Christmas Carol* or Clement Moore's classic poem, *A Visit from St. Nicholas.* Such activities often so quickly become a part of a family's tradition that in a few years no one can remember how or when they began!

Have a happy and creative holiday season and a very Merry Christmas!

SOURCES AND REFERENCES*

A Walk in the Woods:

A Guide to Nature in Winter, by Donald W. Stokes, Little, Brown & Co., Boston, 1976, $8.95. This illustrated book is an excellent guide to trees, cones, pods, weeds, and winter plants used in making decorations.

Wreaths:

Wreath frames of all kinds are available at florist shops, garden centers, and some crafts supply stores.

Adhesive caulking is sold at hardware and home improvement stores.

Unshredded sphagnum moss is available from florists and garden centers.

Decking the Halls:

Thin wires for tying, roping, and securing cones are available at hardware stores and departments.

Quilting thread can be purchased at fabric stores and departments.

Reversible gift wraps are sold at stationery stores.

Cotton craft ribbon is available at fabric and crafts supply stores and often from florists.

Plaster of Paris is sold at hardware and crafts supply stores.

Dowels are sold in a variety of sizes at hardware stores.

Nativity Scenes:

See note at bottom.

Small Gifts To Make:

Potpourri for filling sachets, as well as individual flowers and herbs, is available by mail from Herbitage Farm, RFD 2, Richmond, NH 03470, and from Pickity Place, Mason, NH 03048. Price lists are free from both if you send a stamped, self-addressed envelope.

Lace and trims are available from Homesew, Bethlehem, PA 18018. Send for their free catalog.

Quilt batting is sold at fabric stores and departments.

Bone and metal rings are available at fabric stores and notions counters.

Poster-weight card stock is sold in large sheets at stationery and office supply stores.

Silk and rayon embroidery floss is sold by Folklorico, P.O. Box 625, Ramona Street, Palo Alto, CA 94302. Send a stamped, self-addressed envelope to receive a price list.

Toys To Make:

Millet seed for beanbags is available at health-food stores and wherever birdseed is sold.

The How-to Book of International Dolls, by Loretta Holz, Crown Publishers, Inc., New York, 1980, $12.95. This is an excellent guide to making all kinds of dolls.

Gifts for Children To Make:

Small samples of wallpaper are sometimes available free from home decorating stores. Ask them if they will save an outdated book for you.

The Tree Trims:

Knitting spools are sold in yarn shops.

Florist wire is available in several weights at florist shops.

Invisible thread is available at fabric stores and departments, or you can substitute fine monofilament fishing line, available from sporting-goods stores.

Holiday Entertaining, edited by Georgia Orcutt and Sandra Taylor, Yankee, Inc., Dublin, New Hampshire, 1980, $8.95. Recipes for holiday breads, cakes, cookies, candies, snacks, and beverages; menus (with accompanying recipes) for Christmas dinner; plus ideas for table settings and instructions for building a gingerbread house.

Yankee Home Crafts, by Barbara Radcliffe Rogers, Yankee, Inc., Dublin, New Hampshire, 1979, $9.95. Chapters on growing herbs and flowers especially for potpourri, a number of recipes for potpourri, and directions for additional sachets.

Many of the projects in this book are available in kit form (with all materials) from Herbitage Farm, RFD 2, Richmond, NH 03470. A stamped, self-addressed envelope will bring a complete listing.

Barbara Radcliffe Rogers grew up in New Hampshire in a family with a deep interest in both history and crafts. Her childhood toys were tools and craft materials, and the family stories in the evening concerned times long past. Her own career reflects this heritage of storytellers and craftsmen.

Barbara's past employment is as varied as her present interests: she has been a silversmith, a cooking teacher, an antiques dealer, a speechwriter, an editor, and a legislative assistant to a congressman, among other things. She and her husband travel widely, with a special interest in South America.

She is married to Attorney Stillman Rogers. They live with their two daughters, Julie and Lura, and a changing assortment of animals at Herbitage Farm in Richmond, New Hampshire, where the family runs its own herb business.

Barbara writes for a number of magazines on subjects ranging from cooking and gardening to antiques and handicrafts. In 1979 her book *Yankee Home Crafts* was published.